Work Smarts

Work
Smarts

What CEOs Say
You Need to Know to
Get Ahead

Betty
Liu

WILEY

Even if you're on the right track,
you'll get run over if you just sit there.
—Will Rogers

Contents

Part Four: Things I've Learned

Introduction

Y ou've just graduated college . . .
    You want to get to a promotion . . .
    . . . or you've just been laid off.

Whatever the case, you're looking for some advice. Real advice. What does it *really* take to succeed? How do you get started? How do you pick yourself back up if you've fallen? What if I need to jump-start my career and it's not enough that my spouse or mother is telling me I'm the greatest person in the world. That's not actually getting me to my goal. I need real advice "from the street," so to speak.

If you feel any of the above, this book is for you.

It's also a book for me.

I interview people for a living who are at the top of their careers: CEOs, economists, policy thinkers, entrepreneurs. Inevitably, I began to wonder, how did they get there? Why can't we get beyond the follow-your-passion advice and really find out what it takes to forge a career that maximizes all your interests and skills. What holds people back? What gets them ahead?

No career is perfect. Mine is riddled with mistakes and rejections. That's why I had in the back of my mind that this book is also written for me. Have you ever lain awake at night, rehashing a conversation or a meeting? Yep, that's me. Maybe I didn't convey what I wanted to in the right way, I think. "I shoulda" and "I coulda" are common phrases that pop in my head. When I head into the boss' office to pitch an idea, I fret about it beforehand. How do I say it right? Surely, I think, others go through this too. How do *they* find the advice?

There's a joke that there are more therapists in Manhattan than police. If you widened that out, according to data extrapolated from the International Coaching Federation, there's now about one life coach for every 3,200 people in the United States. A decade ago, who even heard of a life coach? Clearly, people are looking for guidance, especially when they keep hearing about a jobs market that's scarily getting smaller and tougher.

About 9 million people lost their jobs during the latest recession that began in 2007. As of this writing, things have improved. Firings are at their lowest level in five years and job openings are, conversely, at the highest level in five years. But the situation is a lot tougher. Some jobs in manufacturing, autos, and finance may never come back. Our salaries have pretty much gone nowhere in the last 10 years, which means we've got less money to spend because prices keep going up. And while the jobs are coming back, a good number of them are part-time or lower paying jobs which helps bring down the jobless rate, but doesn't do much in the great scheme of getting ahead.

Okay, I'm not trying to depress you. I'm just giving you a reality check. Many people bury their heads in the sand when it comes to their careers. They hope things will just work out. But careers are not a lottery ticket—they're not made out of luck. One CEO told me one of his biggest regrets is not managing his career better when he was younger. And this is coming from someone who is now a multi-millionaire with his own business. He says the biggest mistake he sees others make is that people are too passive about their careers. I'm a big believer in "everything happens for a reason," but at the least, you want to make sure you're doing everything you can to put the odds in your favor.

I'm not *only* talking about big ideas like: "How do I start my own business?" I'm talking about the small things that add up to a successful career:

How to network.
How to ask for a raise.

How to overcome fear.
How to be liked.

Men and women both have problems with the above. Around the time I was writing and researching, Sheryl Sandberg's book *Lean In* sparked a national debate about equality of women in the workplace. I was glad to see all the attention the Facebook chief operating officer brought to the topic but I also felt the impression was that women did everything wrong in the workplace. The fact is, both men and women commit similar blunders. Both feel deficient in many of the topics Sheryl pointed out—networking, mentorship, salaries. I have a male friend who constantly complains he is not well paid. The problem is not his gender but because he's just not very good at asking for a raise.

So if you want to know what's the best way to do this, read this book. If you've ever wanted to get inside a boss' head, this is as close as you'll get. If you're curious to know how the best in business got where they are, read on. If you want to know how even the most successful CEOs out there made mistakes and got fired, that's all in this book, too. Take your head out of the sand and go out there with your eyes wide open and only good will come out of it.

★★★★★★★★

People ask me all the time how I got into television.

The reason why they ask is because I got into television mid-career. I made the switch at the worst possible time, when I had left my job to have children. Not only was I leaving my current job but I was also attempting to get into a new, competitive career after having kids.

I learned two very valuable lessons in my career switch.

One came from a television coach who taught me something that had nothing to do with television. Let me explain.

A television agent said to me (years before I actually left my job) that if I had any serious thoughts about trying my hand at on-air work, I would need to hire a talent coach. So on her recommendation, I found one in New York. It was just a one-day session held at this person's office. Or at least, I think it was her office. It may have been one of those rented spaces that give small businesses the air of a real office.

She walked over and led me into a little white room where several newspapers were laid out. Over the next hour or so, she had me read the newspapers as if they were television scripts. "More energy and emphasis!" she guided. After dozens of reads, I was starting to tune out. How many different ways can I read these paragraphs, I thought. Where I thought I was conveying energy, she was telling me I sounded flat. What was I really trying to accomplish? I just wanted to report good stories; I kept asking myself, why did I need to learn to read? She started getting on my nerves. I started not to like her hair. I wondered if her methods worked. I began to think about her fee. Everything else entered my head except that I needed to focus on being better to get a job.

Sensing my animosity, she suddenly sat down.

"I know this is frustrating," she said. "I'm trying to help you find a job. You're getting mad at me but you're really mad at the process. It's scary out there. Everyone wants to do the same thing you're doing."

She got up and grabbed a black marker and scribbled on the whiteboard.

$$\text{Opportunity} + \text{Preparation} = \text{Luck}$$

"Betty, do you understand what this means?"

"Yes, I do," I said flatly.

"No, do you *really* understand what this means?"

I stared at her for a moment.

"People see other's successes and they think, oh, they're just lucky. Nobody is ever lucky, trust me. Sure, things happen to people. There's stories everywhere of people who've been toiling away and all of a sudden, they get the dream job they've always wanted; or their business idea suddenly takes off and they make millions. We look at that and think, they're lucky. No honey, they're not lucky. They were *prepared*.

"Opportunities are everywhere for people. But if you're not prepared, then you won't be able to capitalize on that opportunity. It's not luck, it's being prepared. It's doing the really hard work of being prepared for the one day when you get that opportunity. It may only come once so you have to be prepared. Your job is to prepare your whole life for that opportunity. Do you understand what I'm saying?"

She leaned in. "Do you understand?"

I hadn't thought I was buying a life lesson but there it was, staring me in the face.

At that point, it really did sink in.

Richard Wiseman is a researcher in the UK who explores the idea of luck. In his fascinating 2003 book *The Luck Factor*, he concocted an experiment to show how "lucky" and "unlucky" people behave.

In one, he taped a five-pound British note on the ground outside a coffee shop near his office. He asked his test subjects, Brenda and Martin, to meet someone involved in a research project at the cafe. Martin considered himself a lucky man. Brenda thought she was an unlucky person. The scheming professor put various people in the coffee shop including a "millionaire" who was to do exactly the same thing with Brenda as he would with Martin.

Can you guess what happened?

Martin spotted the money right away on the ground, picked it up, and walked into the coffee shop. He sat next to the "millionaire" and began chatting him up, even buying him a coffee with the extra money he found. They began a fruitful dialogue and discussed connecting again on possible projects. Brenda, in the meantime, walked right past the free money, bought her coffee, and also sat down next to the millionaire. But she didn't talk to him and he was instructed not to approach her first. So she left with no interaction and no extra money.

Imagine this was a real life scenario and you can easily see how one set of behaviors could lead to a lucky break and the other would lead to nothing. How many millionaires have you walked by and not said a word?

Me, personally, I really don't like the word lucky. I prefer "optimism." The people featured in this book are generally resilient optimists. They're always preparing for the next chance that could change their futures. In certain cases, a no means a no, but in this instance, when it comes to your career, a no means you've got to look for another avenue to a yes.

After that day with the talent coach I stopped deluding myself that if I didn't get a job in television it was because I was unlucky. I went about practicing and preparing and keeping my ears and eyes peeled for any opportunities or chance connections. I wasn't nutty about it but just conscious that this was my goal and I was going to somehow get to it one way or the other.

Which led me to the other valuable lesson I learned in this transition.

Persistence does pay off.

It would be a nicely tied story if I said I got my job in television a few months later.

No, I had much longer to go. I spent many years after with other coaches. I auditioned for several jobs with nothing. Lots of people were more than happy to tell me I had no future in television. I remember one executive producer who said he had a good gut sense of who had innate talent for television and he didn't see it in me. I heard a few years later he got laid off.

To learn the art of scriptwriting, I joined a public radio station. I knew it would teach me how to write differently and to really understand what on-air reading was like. I didn't get paid and I didn't care. What they were teaching me was far more valuable. I put together a professional demo tape. I spent many hours and lots of money getting it just right. The tape editors I worked with were all freelance guys who were very nice, but eager to go on about how ruthless television was and that people end up getting fired and tossed out like yesterday's garbage. There was a lot of tuning out during this time. If I listened to all the negativity, I would have given up pretty quickly.

Years later, when I could have been written off, on maternity leave, and with no job to come back to, I got the call. The head of CNBC Asia, a woman who I had met years earlier and who did not hire me then, said she finally had a job opening and thought of me. I don't know why she thought of me, but she did. I had the right background. She seemed to like me. I kept in touch with her through the years with an occasional e-mail.

A few months later, I was packing my bags and heading back to Hong Kong in my first on-air television job. I was nervous, excited, and scared but also grateful. I was glad she didn't hire me back then. I wasn't prepared and she knew it. I was ready now. Later, whenever friends said to me, you're so lucky you got that job, I would think, *you don't even know the half of it.*

I don't even remember this television coach's name—or her face. I'm sure if I really tried, I could track her down. But I like having what she taught me hang nameless, like a broad script in the sky. She set me on that path of preparation and I learned persistence.

So if you still think a successful career is much about luck, stop reading. If not, read ahead so you can *be prepared.*

Part One

If I Knew This Before, I'd Be a Millionaire . . .

Chapter 1

The Company of One

Glenn Hutchins talks really fast. He's also really tall. The combination of the two means he's good at making a deal and he could have played basketball.

So when Glenn made his riches in private equity, he bought a stake in a basketball team, the Boston Celtics. Glenn graduated from Harvard and began his career on Wall Street as a junior analyst at Chemical Bank, working—literally—in the basement. It wasn't long before he catapulted up the food chain and built a $13 billion private equity firm.

On the day I went to visit him in his office, he was his usual amused and amusing self, padding around the place in his socks (he said he'd just been to the dentist which, at least to him, explained why he was shoeless). In the hallway were the remnants of a buffet lunch, which made me feel as if I'd arrived at the party just a little too late. Glenn being in socks only added to that.

"We do this everyday for our associates," Glenn said, pointing to the salmon swimming in cooling mango salsa juices.

"That's a nice touch," I replied, grabbing a plate of the leftovers and heading to the private dining room adjoining Glenn's office.

For some reason, giving employees free food is an instant morale booster. Perhaps because the profit margin for a person is 100 percent. As in, this is *free*, so I have 100 percent gotten my value out of this product, whatever it may be. There's a familiar saying in journalism that if you want reporters to show up at a press conference, just lay out free food and even better, some free alcohol.

Before long, Glenn and I began talking about his career and like many of the people in this book, he was absolutely confident in his belief on what makes a successful career.

"You can choose one of two career journeys. One resembles a canyon where you coast downhill in your early years and then spend your midlife, when tuition and mortgage payments come due, trudging out. The other is more like a mountain, which is a steep and arduous climb in your thirties and forties but which then frees you later in life to have time for family, philanthropy, and service."

He then went on to tell me about his early years at Chemical Bank and how the traders on the floors above him snubbed their noses at the geeky analyst.

"I suppose I was a bit of a nerd, and as a result, I was relegated to the unglamorous credit department," he said.

"So what did you do?" I asked.

"Though I learned an enormous amount . . . I couldn't get promoted because I was in the back office. So I went instead to Harvard, did my JD and MBA . . . it strikes me as better for all involved to harness the talents of young people rather than restrain and discourage them."

Many people would describe someone like Glenn as a Wall Street guy. But I see something else—I see an entrepreneur. Yes, he did eventually start his own business. But even before starting his firm, Silver Lake Partners, Glenn already thought of himself as his own entity. His own company of *one*. Others didn't get the value of this company, but he did and he grew it to success.

This is something I found to be one of the biggest distinguishing factors between the leaders and the followers, the CEO and the rest of us. Most of the people who are successful are either entrepreneurs or have an entrepreneurial mindset, even if they worked at the same company for decades. There were exceptions to the rule, but not a lot. Being a "company of one" is not a selfish mindset, but rather a healthy one. People who have this mindset are optimists, they're more productive, feel more confident because they know their own value and it can't be taken away.

What exactly is this mindset? Quite literally at the basic level, being a company of one is striking out on your own. For example, company X doesn't get who you really are, everybody around you has blinders on and you would do a much better job just building your own company than to stay at company X for another 5, 10, 15 years. In other words, you're like Glenn. Or in another example, you're bored with being a corporate lawyer and the midlife crisis hits, which means six months later, you're baking cupcakes at your own shop and you're 10 times happier than when you were pushing papers charging $500 an hour. That's easily being the company of one.

But more often than not, the company-of-one mindset is about freeing yourself from the idea that your job is your career. Your job is your avenue to a career, so long as the job and the career match. Sadly, it often doesn't. But people who have this mindset are easy to spot. They always have a few projects going on. This person may be a marketing executive by day, but at night she's writing a book. Or he's working at IBM, but in his spare time, loves producing how-to videos on YouTube. They're creative people.

Jeff Hayzlett literally was a marketing executive by day. He was the chief marketing officer at Kodak when he decided to leave and pursue his own projects. When I told him about this company-of-one mindset, he immediately got it.

"Brand of one," he said over lunch at the Manhattan eatery, Tao.

He said he had about 40-plus projects going on at the same time, including a gig at Bloomberg Television as a contributing editor. He'd been a judge on NBC's *Celebrity Apprentice*. He consults and advises companies on marketing and public relations but his biggest business is himself.

"I make the most from the speaking," he said.

When I ask him what his brand is, he says he's unabashedly one of the best marketers out there and a cowboy to boot. He advised me social media was most important in developing your own brand. He grabbed his iPad and showed me all the tweets he'd scheduled later in the afternoon, tomorrow, next week, and even next *year*.

"Whatever you have, put it out there and let it echo," he said. And as if to drive home the point, he tweeted out to me after our lunch. I barely had a chance to figure out how to make my way back to the office and he'd already tweeted a note saying thanks for the lunch for all the twittersphere to see.

Sam Zell, the self-made billionaire real estate investor, said his entrepreneurial zeal might have been because he was "born 90 days after my parents' arrival in the United States [from Poland]."

"I had the opportunity to watch my parents, as immigrants, deal with significant changes and challenges," Sam says, relaxing in his Manhattan apartment. "And as I watched that, and I think about it, among the things that have made my career so unique are those common denominators of change and challenge.

"The ultimate definition of an entrepreneur is someone who is always thinking he can do things a different, better way. If he walks down the street and sees a painter on a ladder, he thinks, 'Gee, if he'd moved the ladder to the middle of the wall, then he could paint both sides without having to go up and down the ladder as many times,'" he said. "I can't tell you why I think that way, but that's literally the way I think all the time. It's always been that way. I look at things and see them differently than other people do.

"In my career, I've been industry agnostic. There aren't a lot of investors who have been in rail car leasing, container leasing, electrical distribution, waste energy, bicycles, natural gas, food additive manufacturing, logistics, and myriad other industries. I'm very much like a private equity guy is today except that I've always been a private equity guy—with my own private equity."

Later, I thought about what Sam said. My parents did not come from Poland but from China. My father may have chosen a safe profession as a doctor but he pursued it with the same kind of risk that entrepreneurs do. My relatives all thought he was crazy to move to a country whose language he did not know, to try to practice medicine in a system that did not recognize his medical training, and to do all this with barely any savings to his name and three people—my mother, my sister, and myself—to support. At age 40, he arrived in the United States with $30 in his pocket, no job, and a fierce determination to make things work.

Martin Sorrell also waited until he was a 40 to start his own business. Martin is a punchy, outspoken advertising executive who founded WPP, one of the world's largest advertising agencies, which earned him a knighthood in his native Britain. On his shield he has inscribed in Latin his motto: *Celeritas et Perseverantia* (Persistence and Speed).

"I probably could have [started my company] at thirty-five," he tells me. "There are people who are good at running companies but not starting companies and I wanted to do both . . . I didn't want to start a rinky-dink company. I only own two percent of the company or a little bit under two percent which, to me, is a lot of money, but to some others, they think that's chicken poop. But rather than owning, say eighty percent of something smaller, I'm quite happy to have two percent of something that's much, much bigger."

When I looked up later the public information on WPP, I learned Martin is worth about $350 million just on his shares alone in the company he founded.

On the entrepreneurial mindset, Martin said: "Founders have different, I think, emotional connections to what they do. I mean, if you're a hired hand or a turnaround expert, your loyalty and emotional commitment to the company that you're running is different than if you started it . . . you just think differently. There was a famous football manager in the UK called Bill Shankly who was the manager of the Liverpool football club . . . this was when they were very successful. And he said, 'Football is not a matter of life and death. It's more important than that.' So WPP is not a matter of life and death—it's more important than that. So just like Berkshire Hathaway for Warren Buffett or JPMorgan for Jamie Dimon, it's as much a part of them, you could argue, as their family. Their family probably comes first, but it's as much a part of them as their family."

When I looked up the quote later, the official line from Shankly went more like: "Some people believe football is a matter of life and death, I am very disappointed with that attitude. I can assure you it is much, much more important than that."

"I wear this jersey and I *bleed* this blood," Jamie Dimon told me a few months later at his headquarters in midtown Manhattan. "I feel responsible for our 250,000–plus employees. I wouldn't leave here and do something else at another corporation . . . I'm very proud of our company and I want every employee to be proud of it."

If there is a bank CEO who has his own brand of one, Jamie Dimon does. He was revered during the 2007–2008 financial crisis as the one leader who did not come under fire for bad management. While fellow CEOs were succumbing to their own bad decisions, Jamie looked like the smartest guy in the room. *Time* magazine named him to the world's 100 most influential people list in 2008, 2009, and 2011. He was called CEO of the year by *Institutional Investor*, a finance-focused magazine, in 2011.

When I met him, he had just been through one of the toughest years of his career at JPMorgan. Regulators, the press, and critics were all hounding him over the so-called London Whale trading scandal where some bad trades at a London office cost the firm more than $6 billion. The event even has its own Wikipedia page. I could tell the situation really hit Jamie personally. He said he spent a weekend writing out his annual letter to shareholders to give his final thoughts on the scandal. He told me he wrote the letter by himself with no edits—it was a letter from him personally to everyone.

Even though he didn't start JPMorgan—the bank says it was founded in 1799 as The Manhattan Company and at one point in its complicated history, it was called Chemical Bank (yes, the same Chemical Bank that did not promote Glenn Hutchins)—Jamie helped build the firm after its 2004 merger with Bank One, where he was chief executive. In other words, the JPMorgan of today is largely Jamie Dimon's vision.

"I see our executives, they get in the elevators, I always say hi. I have administrative town halls, they all call me Jamie. They all know me. They'll pat me on the back, 'Hey you!' The mailroom guys will say hi to me.

"There are some companies where executives have their own elevator. You cannot send that message to your people. I remember getting into an elevator once and the employees were talking about me. I said, 'I'm back here!'"

"That really happened?" I asked.

"Yeah, they didn't know I was in the back. I don't know if what they were saying about me was good or bad. I just wanted to give them a heads up."

The way Jamie talked about his company was with the same affection I heard from Martin and Sam, and would later hear from Warren Buffett. All had a solid foundation of who they were, their own companies and brands, and that translated into their companies. When you start something that is your own, when you control and own your own destiny, it's not just life and death. It's more important than that.

★★★★★★★★

The fact is, most people would love to be like Sam—their own boss. According to an Edward Jones survey in 2012, 70 percent of workers liked the idea of being entrepreneurs at work. But only a puny 15 percent thought they had what it takes to be one. The biggest fear preventing people from pursuing their entrepreneurial dreams was the loss of their savings. The second biggest fear is essentially the same thing: a lack of support or safety net if they failed. None of this is surprising but then again, it's not surprising that many people feel they're stuck in a career rut.

Graham Weston is another billionaire entrepreneur (eventually in my world of business news, billionaires pop up like weeds) who recently co-authored a book called *Unstoppables*. The book is about creating more self-made business owners in the country and in the foreword, Graham recalls how he went back to his alma mater of Texas A&M University to give a talk.

"After offering a few remarks, I asked the students 'How many of you would like to start your own businesses one day, or work for a young business?' Practically every hand shot up," Graham writes. "Then I asked 'And how many of you will be doing that as soon as you graduate from A&M?' There were a few chuckles around the room, and nearly all the hands came down. It seems there was a huge gap between the dream of entrepreneurship and the real-life plans most students had created."

I have never owned or run my own business, but any profession, including journalism, can have entrepreneurial aspects to it. I create things and that means finding my own stories and creating my own show. I have always worked for myself even though I have never once worked on my own. In television news, it's important to be part of a large network with the resources and the distribution to be seen by the widest possible audience. But even that may change as journalists begin to think more like entrepreneurs. And entrepreneurs like Reed Hastings of Netflix, Jeff Bezos of Amazon, and others begin to change the way television is delivered, period.

What's the driving force behind entrepreneurial tendencies? Jay Samit, a serial entrepreneur who has created ooVoo, one of the fastest-growing apps rivaling Skype, joked: "Maybe because my mother never hugged me enough when I was a kid. I'm always seeking approval from others." No surprise that I learned later Jay studied to be a journalist at UCLA.

Jay is a slim, boyish-looking guy in his fifties who shoots back and forth from New York to Los Angeles, where he not only runs his company but also teaches at the University of Southern California. Jay has both worked for himself and also rose up the senior ranks as a music executive at Universal, Sony, and EMI. He described back to me the company of one concept.

"What a person should do is realize that they have to be a brand of one. They're going to have to reinvent themselves and their skill set nonstop. Think of a doctor that's my age. That means they got out of medical school twenty-five years ago. The majority of drugs, treatments, machines—everything is completely different, right? There's nothing that's done the same as when they got out of school. So if a doctor didn't keep on being a lifelong learner, they couldn't be a doctor. Well, that's the same for a cook, a graphic artist, and an advertising executive—name your field. Journalists that thought they would get a lifelong thing writing for a newspaper—they're gone."

"What's your brand?" I ask.

"My brand is 'you've got a problem and I can help solve it.' No one ever hired me for my looks, right?" he said, chuckling.

Jay told me he has two rules for his managers to encourage entrepreneurial thinking.

"Every direct report that I've had for at least the past fifteen years I give the following two rules to, okay? You don't work for me, I work for you. My job is to give you the resources that you need to do your job."

"Do they believe you?" I ask.

"Sometimes yes and sometimes no. Rule number two makes it very clear. If you work for me for a year and you do not make a mistake, I will fire you."

I look a little surprised. "And you've done that?"

"Oh yeah, I do. [Being] an entrepreneur is not for the faint of heart. The perfect kid that stayed up all through school and got the perfect grade and has the stomach in knots is not cut out for this. They can't handle failing and the humiliation."

I make a mental note to myself about how many nights I tossed and turned, worried about getting straight A's on my report cards. I'm pretty sure if Jay and I had been classmates he would have been the bad ass in the back while I was the uptight, Little Miss Perfect A's in the front.

Other managers may not go to such extremes as Jay, but you get the point.

Do Entrepreneurs Perform Better Than Outsiders?

When you start investing in yourself and your own business, chances are you'll do a much better job.

Yes, there are plenty of stories where entrepreneurs almost destroyed their own companies. Not because they didn't love their own creations, but because they just stunk at being business leaders. A few names come to mind: Andrew Mason, who founded Groupon, and Mark Pincus, who built Zynga, the online gaming company. For a while, it seemed Mark Zuckerberg might be Facebook's own worst enemy until he grew up and started acting more like a CEO.

The *Harvard Business Review* released a survey in 2013 that calculated who were the best performing CEOs during their tenures. No surprise, two entrepreneurs topped the list.

Steve Jobs.

Jeff Bezos.

Jeff is his own company of one. He went left when others went right. Not many people remember, but Jeff started off as a banker. But he always loved building and dismantling things and that's what led him to eventually start Amazon. He began the company while he was literally moving—driving across the country. When others told him his idea couldn't be done, he did it, starting off 24/7 in his garage.

The editor-in-chief of the *Harvard Business Review*, Adi Ignatius, did a rare interview with Jeff for the survey issue. And one of the best examples about what it takes to be a company of one was in this answer: "Inventing and pioneering require a willingness to be misunderstood for long periods of time. One of the early examples of this was the customer reviews. One wrote to me and said, 'You don't understand your business. You make money when you sell things. Why do you allow these negative customer reviews?'

"And when I read that letter, I thought, 'We don't make money when we sell things. We make money when we help customers make purchase decisions.'"

It was a cold-cock simple idea that, today, almost every single online retailer has copied.

As I mentioned, there's usually two ways a person finally discovers their company of one. In the first, there is such a burning desire to do something, you can't ignore it. You're miserable until you satisfy this inner yearning. Jim Reynolds, the CEO of a boutique investment bank, told me that he was the best bond salesman in the Midwest for Merrill Lynch before he left it all to start his own firm. He was good at his job and making a lot of money. But instead of being happy about the future, it looked frightful.

"I really began to get a little bit afraid that I would sit there on the desk, stay on the bond desk, move up to head of fixed income, but still not accomplish the things I knew I was capable of," he said. "I got really scared. I said, 'Jim you could do so many more things, but you're scared to leave here, but you should do those things, they're inside of you.' Eventually, the fear reversed itself—I developed a larger fear of staying there not realizing my potential than the fear I had of walking away from my career. Once that happened, I was off to the races."

He left with half a million dollars from Merrill Lynch to start his own firm, which sounds like a lot of money except when you are trying to compete with companies that have billions of dollars and thousands of bankers. As luck would have it, an old friend of his from decades ago heard he wanted to start his own business. His friend was now the vice chairman of First Chicago Bank.

"I needed a line of credit and he said, 'Okay' and approved me for a two-and-a-half million dollar credit line just on a business plan. Every one of his lending officers and senior people in the bank said do not lend this man the money. We did not have any revenue, I didn't even have a business. I barely had an office, there was nothing but a business plan. He said to his team, 'Give Jim Reynolds the money.' They kept saying 'Jim can take that dough and not do anything with it and just move to Jamaica.' But he said, 'Give Jim that money.'"

Today, Jim has offices all over the country and over 200 employees. He's even helped a president get elected from Chicago as one of the first fundraisers and financial advisors to Barack Obama.

The second way you discover your inner entrepreneur is not exactly the way you want to do it. You get fired. You have a falling out with the company. You're forced to retire. Suddenly you ask yourself, what am I going to do? Essentially, the safety net is taken away and your darkest fears are now sunning themselves in a lounge chair in front of you. Holy crap it's all about *me* and what *I'm* going to do about the future.

Many people do well eventually. They get back on their feet. Either they really do strike out on their own or they join a company again with the experience of knowing what it means to have things taken away. Sometimes that makes people stronger.

Other times, it makes them more afraid. The times that it makes people more afraid is when they had tied up their own value in their jobs and not in themselves—their own company of one. They don't believe in the value of their own company. I've seen it too many times and I'm sure you have too.

****

So how does an entrepreneur—a person who believes in his or her own brand—really think?

Successful entrepreneurs look at the world a little differently than the rest of us.

Where others see roadblocks, *they* see opportunities. When someone says you can't, they say why not. When they have $10 to their name, they double down.

Short of getting directly inside their heads, a few of the entrepreneurs I talked to revealed their strategic thinking.

Sam Zell, as I mentioned, earned his reputation in many businesses but he became a business legend during the peak of the real estate boom. At that time, in February 2007, he sold a group of office buildings for almost $40 billion. Two years later, several of those buildings were underwater from the recession, meaning they were worth less than the loans. Sam sniffed that something in the air wasn't right and he timed his exit perfectly.

Sam said to me: "I virtually codified the phrase: Buying below replacement cost. When I started buying distressed real estate in 1974, I realized I was buying an apartment project for $10,000 a unit, which it cost $14,000 to build each unit originally and it cost about $17,000 to build it in 1974. So I was going to be competing with a developer next door with a building that costs half of what his new building would cost, which meant I could charge lower rents, and get the same, if not better, returns. And if he didn't build that new building, then I was even better off because there would be less supply and the same demand. Buying below replacement cost is a basic, simple premise. There's nothing esoteric about it."

From that thinking—buy below replacement cost—Sam got rich. He called the concept "cold-cock simple." It's a terrifically valuable lesson to learn. Know the value of the thing you're buying. Maybe you can only apply Sam's view in real estate but imagine if you went into every real estate transaction thinking the same thing: How much would it cost to replace this apartment unit or house? If the cost is much more, then you know you have a good deal on your hands. If not, then you need to do some more investigating to make sure it's the right purchase.

Elon Musk described another way of thinking, but it was very similar to Sam's view. Elon is the head of two companies—electric-car maker Tesla and rocket-ship manufacturer SpaceX. He's one of the few CEOs you could also legitimately call an inventor. Borrowing from his physics degree, Elon said he "reasons by first principles."

"It's where you take the most fundamental truths in an area or the things that seem to be the fundamental truths, and you reason up from there to a conclusion. You don't reason by analogy. Most people reason by analogy."

I asked him to give me an example.

"Okay, so reasoning by analogy, like in the rocket business, you would say: So how much have rockets cost? Well, on average they've cost, let's say, $100 million. So, therefore, your rocket will cost $100 million. Now, reasoning from first principles, you would say: What is a rocket made of? What are the engines made of? How are they constructed? The materials, manufacturing processes, all that, and you build that up to say, 'Okay, well, what could a rocket cost if it was done right?' And then you find, 'Oh, wow, a rocket could cost like one-tenth of that.' . . . The problem is that people are putting rockets together in really dumb ways. And then you just have to be a detective and get rid of the dumb ways and then it's much better.

"It's very difficult to make inroads into a new area when reasoning by analogy, because analogies are referencing the past . . . reasoning by analogy is basically copying what others do with very minor incremental changes, and not actually understanding why that thing was even successful in the first place. Most of our life is reasoning by analogy."

"Almost every part?" I ask.

"Yes. You wouldn't be able to get through the day if you try to reason from first principles with everything. It would be just total gridlock. You'd be stuck. You apply it only where it's really important, like if you're trying to create a company or product and then you just have to apply your maximum critical thinking."

To put it in its simplest terms, reasoning by first principles is about defying conventional thinking. Being the annoying little kid who asks "Why?" when parents just want to shut you up and say, "That's just the way it is."

As both Elon and Sam could agree, conventional thinking is the death of any business and entrepreneur. When you start thinking of yourself as a brand and exercising your entrepreneurial thoughts, conventional wisdom is necessarily thrown out the window.

"I think conventional wisdom is one of the greatest horrors of all time," Sam said.

★★★★★★★★

That real estate deal in 2007 helped make Sam one of the wealthiest people in this country. According to *Forbes*, he is the 103rd richest man in America.

As an entrepreneur, he has a lot of company on these lists of billionaires. I noticed that among the richest in the world, many are founders of their own businesses. For example, according to the Bloomberg Billionaires Index:

#5 Ingvar Kamprad: The founder of the furniture retailer Ikea. Net worth: $48.5 billion.
#16 Jeff Bezos: The founder of Amazon. Net worth: $26.6 billion.
#40 Phil Knight: The co-founder of Nike. Net worth: $16.7 billion.
#98 Azim Premji: The co-founder of Wipro, India's third-biggest software exporter. Net worth: $10.6 billion (and apparently he also flies coach 60 to 65 times a year).
Note: These numbers are through July 2013.

Out of the top 100 billionaires ranked by Bloomberg, 27 inherited their wealth. The rest were all self-made.

Out of all who made their own money, 30 were American. That means 43 people outside the United States also created their wealth from nothing—billionaires from India to China to Spain to Mexico. If there's one thing people like to emulate about us, it's the American dream of building something up from nothing.

One who consistently ranks atop these lists is the man Martin mentioned earlier: Warren Buffett. He is always either the second or third richest man, behind his best friend and fellow entrepreneur, Bill Gates.

I've been interviewing Buffett for a few years and attending his massive Berkshire Hathaway shareholders meetings. More than 35,000 people attend and the entire weekend is a festival for investors. There are parties at night, special events during the day, with the highlight being the daylong meeting where Buffett and his longtime partner, Charlie Munger, sit on a stage answering questions ranging from where he expects gold to trade to why taxes should be raised. I've never seen a CEO have as much fun as Buffett does on the day of his shareholders meeting. In 2013, with the song blaring rock-concert loud, he *Y-M-C-A*'ed his way to the stage.

"Why do I love what I'm doing? Well, it's a game that I've spent my life playing and I enjoy it just like a pro golfer would who's been playing golf all his life," Buffett told me. "I'm on my back and I'm Michelangelo painting the Sistine Chapel ceiling or something. And maybe nobody else does, but I get to paint my own painting. And if the board of directors said to me, 'You're using too much red paint, why don't you use more blue paint?' I would probably hand them the brush and tell them what they could do with it anatomically."

Since the 1960s, his company has served as an incubator for other entrepreneurs. He buys companies—like Dairy Queen, See's Candies, Fruit of the Loom, NetJets—and brings them into his fold where they get both advice and money to grow. Every time I talk with a Berkshire CEO, he or she says the best thing about working for Buffett is that he leaves them alone.

"They've got to be in love with the business. When I hand somebody $100 million, or a billion, or $5 billion, and then they hand me the stock certificate, I'm counting on them to run it," he said.

"We never rely on contracts. It wouldn't mean anything. You know, six months later the guy's getting up at six in the morning, and his wife says, 'You know, what the hell are you doing?' He says, 'Oh, I'm getting up to work for some company in Omaha,' and she says, 'I thought the last thirty years we've been building this thing, and now we've got billions of dollars, why aren't we out on a boat, or taking trips to Europe or whatever?' And unless his answer is, 'I'm doing this because I love it,' but he says, 'I'm doing this because I signed an agreement,' you know, it isn't going to work over time. But if he says, 'I'm doing this because I'd rather do it than anything else in the world,' then we're going to have a wonderful leader. . . . I try to buy companies where the managers of them feel that way about their company, and then it's up to me not to destroy that feeling. I can't put it in somebody that it's not in already, but I can destroy it if it's not in there."

Buffett is known for keeping things simple. He has spent the last several decades telling the investing public that the simplest way to get rich in stocks is buying what you like and stick to it. When he announced he was helping candy company Mars fund the acquisition of Wm. Wrigley, the chewing gum company, for $23 billion in 2008, Buffett said he'd been taste-testing the product since he was seven years old and liked it. At the time he said, "I understand a Wrigley or a Mars a whole lot better than I understand the balance sheet of some of the big banks. I know what I'm getting in this, and some of the larger financial institutions, I really don't know what's there."

Sam also keeps it simple.

"Guts and instinct are all simplicity," Sam said. "I went to Harvard Business School in 1988, and I spoke to three hundred of them and I just beat the sh*t out of them, and I said, 'You guys have been sitting here and listening to this concept that everything has a formula, that there's a numeric solution for everything, that as long as you knew that X plus Y. . . . *Bullsh*t!* It's all about what's simple. What's the shortest distance between two points? It's a straight line.'

"That afternoon, to make my point, I said, 'Let me tell you a story and it's a story about Avi and Sarah. And Avi and Sarah were both sixty years old. And on their sixtieth birthdays they decided they were going to take separate vacations. And so Avi, he went to Miami Beach, and Sarah, she went to San Diego. And after about three weeks comes a postcard from Avi. He says, 'Dear Sarah, I'm having a wonderful time. The sun, the surf, the hotel, it's really terrific. And as a matter of fact, I was sitting by the pool today and a twenty-year-old girl walked by. I said hello. She said hello. I asked her to sit down. She sat down. We talked. We swam. We had lunch together. And tonight, she's coming to my suite for a candlelight dinner. Who knows? I may get lucky. Love, Avi.'

"So about three weeks later comes back a postcard from Sarah. 'Dear Avi, I, too, am having a wonderful time. The sun, the surf, the hotel, it's really terrific. As a matter of fact, I was sitting by the pool today when a twenty-year-old guy walked by. I said hello. He said hello. I asked him to sit down. He sat down. We talked. We swam. We had lunch. And tonight he's coming to my suite for a candlelight dinner. Who knows? I may get lucky. Love, Sarah.' And then at the bottom she put a P.S., and she said, 'Avi, you shouldn't forget that twenty goes into sixty a lot more times than sixty goes into twenty.' [*laughing*] Now, the numbers are the same, but what they mean is drastically different!"

"What kind of reaction did you get?" I asked.

"Oh, they fell over. I mean, you know, the girls all got embarrassed. Nobody goes to Harvard and gives a serious speech, and then hits them between the eyes like that. But it's all about thou shall not take oneself seriously. Does that make the point?"

And it did—*keep it simple* and don't overthink. Sometimes the best strategies are the simplest ones.

★★★★★★★★

"Keep it simple" is what Graham Weston would call a *micro-script* that you keep in your head every time you confront a challenge. So if you have a great idea and want to pursue it, you keep chanting in your head "keep it simple, keep it simple, keep it simple" so you don't over-complicate your overall goal.

As Graham points out in his book, we all have these micro-scripts in our head.

"Don't drink and drive."

"There's no substitute for hard work."

"Every no gets me closer to a yes."

In 1992, David Mamet brought us probably one of the best micro-scripts to hit the big screen in *Glengarry Glen Ross*. Alec Baldwin as the "I-made-$970,000-last-year" Blake, flipping the white board and spitting out:

Always
Be
Closing

Who could forget the famous line? "Nice guy? I don't give a sh*t. Good father? F*ck you! Go home and play with your kids. You wanna work here? *Close!*"

Now, while that micro-script turned the office into a seed of deception and debauchery, a similar one is what turns people into hard-driving, successful entrepreneurs.

Always
Be
Moving

Time and again, entrepreneurs told me that to get from what Sam Zell described as "A to B" is to keep moving. Graham and his co-author Bill Schley wrote about their 80/20 rule: "Spend 20 percent or less of your time pondering and preparing, and 80 percent or more *doing*—repeatedly." In describing the Law of Motion, they quote Isaac Newton's first law which states an object in motion stays in motion.

Three hundred years later, baseball great Yogi Berra said, "If you come to a fork in the road, take it."

"What I usually share with women is, why is it on a weekend we wait to have the kitchen spotless and perfect and dishes put away before we enjoy the day?" Sheila Marcelo, the founder of Care.com, the fastest-growing caregiving company in the country tells me. "Guys, on the other hand, would just say 'Let's go for it. I don't care if the bed's not made. Let's get out of here.' There's this sense that everything has to be in place and orderly and it's the same in our careers. We think that we *have* to have all the experience. We need to know this and that and everything before we jump in and run something."

Always **B**e **M**oving, but not, as General Colin Powell wrote in his book, *It Worked for Me*, where you're moving around like a "busy bastard." There are plenty of people who are busy. They fill their schedules up with busy things, they stay late in the office doing lots of busy things, their weekends are filled up with busy activities, but the problem is none of those activities get them anywhere. Often, people are busy when they have no idea where they are truly going. Or they are busy because they don't really want to face what they want to do.

I have encountered many people like this and I'm sure you have, too. It may be clear to you that they should be moving, but instead they are moving in all the wrong directions. One person I know has been talking so long about his desire to move into another profession but every year passes and he still has not done anything about it. Instead, he jumps from job to job in his existing profession, hoping that the next job is going to bring the satisfaction that he seeks. And of course, it never does. I keep hearing, "After this, I plan to make the leap" but I feel sorry that it may never happen and 10 years down the road, it will be too late.

Another person I know has always wanted to open up her own business. She has the training for it and the right experience. But she continues to work for other people, piling on more and more hours because she keeps spending beyond her means. She bought a big house. She buys gifts for everyone, including for people who will likely never buy her a gift back. She goes on fancy vacations. She's spending all her money, which is keeping her busy and exhausted, but doing nothing for what she really wants. Not surprisingly, she is unhappy with her state in life and can't figure how to get out of it.

When I lived in Atlanta, one year I put all my energy into writing a book about the South. I spent six weeks traveling around the region, recording how the area was developing. One Mississippi woman let me stay at her house for a few days to get to know her family. Another person—a musician—spent a few days in Louisiana immersing me in Zydeco music. In Selma, Alabama, I became a fixture for a week, staying at a bed and breakfast, talking ghost stories with the bartender. I was doing what I thought was real, narrative journalism. I asked for six months off from *the Financial Times* and they graciously gave it to me to write it all out.

And then I sat down to write it. And write. I spent six months in my little home office staring at the computer screen. I went to the coffee shop and instead of writing, I read lots of magazines. There were days I said, "Today I will write" and it wasn't until 10 P.M. that I would trundle off to my office to write. And by then, I was too tired.

I did manage to write about 35,000 words but I knew the book wasn't very good. There were parts I liked about it, but overall, it was weighed down by all my insecurities. The writing was not very confident. Instead of enjoying the process, it was like I was putting myself through water torture. To my full expectation, every literary agent rejected the manuscript. Truth be told, I wasn't very disappointed by the rejection letters. I was just disappointed in the whole process and myself. I still have all the notes, recordings, manuscript in—where else—my parent's basement.

I describe the above as an example of when fear, which everyone has, keeps you from moving in the right direction. I had a fear the manuscript wouldn't be very good and so . . . it wasn't very good. I couldn't stop that nagging voice telling me I had no right to write about this subject. The other people I mentioned are all snagged by a similar fear—a fear of failing—which prevents them from moving forward.

Always Be Moving is about moving forward in every direction that gets you to your goal. It doesn't matter if you fail. It doesn't matter if your idea gets stolen. It only matters that you continually work towards what you want, whether it's starting your own business or moving up in your own company.

"So many people think it's about having a brilliant idea. Nothing could be further than the truth. The idea is not to take your idea and nurture it and save it and savor it and water it. The idea is to kill your idea," Jay Samit says.

"What?" I ask.

"*Kill* your idea. What can you do to destroy this idea? This idea will fail. This idea is the worst idea, and here's why, and as you keep on knocking and attacking that idea, what survives, what comes out of that furnace is hardened and can survive competition and defend itself.

"At the end of the day," Jay says. "As [Thomas] Edison said, 'It's one percent inspiration, ninety-nine percent perspiration.'"

★★★★★★★★

Rachael Ray is the lively, effusive cooking star and daytime talk show host who made famous in kitchens across America the acronym, EVOO (extra virgin olive oil). When I first began to seriously learn how to cook, I remember tuning into Rachael's *30 Minute Meals* Food Network show and thinking, who is this woman? I loved watching how easy she made two or three dishes in 30 minutes. And she always had a big, girly sense of humor about it.

Years later when I started doing television, I appreciated how hard it is to make things look easy on television. The amount of work that goes into a half-hour cooking program is enormous. I joke that in television, everyone works hard so you—the viewer—can relax.

In the spring of 2013, I met Rachael at a taping of one of our primetime programs, *Titans at the Table*. In fact, the whole entourage of Food Network stars were there, including Bobby Flay and Mario Batali. What we ate was decidedly un-gourmet—fried fish, burgers, fries, hummus, and other pub fare. Bobby kept asking me if I knew where the fish came from on my plate, which instantly made me paranoid. He later explained from a chef's point of view, you should never order fish when you don't know the name of it. Lesson learned.

It was fun to see the chefs out of their kitchens. Rather than exchange recipes and cooking tips, the conversation turned to what made them all big brands. How did they go from essentially kitchen cooks to their own companies of one?

At one point, I turned to Rachael and asked her what was a break-through moment.

"There was no breakthrough," she replied. "My life has been a series of happy accidents. And I think that the thing that has made those accidents successful is that I enjoy working really, *really* hard. I enjoy a long day. I enjoy many plates in the air . . . I think you should always get up with the intent to make yourself better and to grow and to learn."

I point this out because this is the last part of what I found most in common amongst entrepreneurs and what is key to a company of one mindset.

You have to work hard.

It sounds obvious but it may surprise you how many people believe others rise to the top for so many reasons other than putting in the time. There may be cases where some lazy jerk gets ahead but who wants to put in the effort to discover why. The most surefire way to get what you want is to work hard at it.

Warren Buffett says he wants his CEOs to have a fire burning in them for the business. Every entrepreneur's war stories begin with sleepless nights in a parents' basement or at the office, working nonstop on an idea.

Elon Musk says he was born with such drive to do everything it took to succeed that when he was five, he walked for "ten, fifteen miles" to his cousin's house, which his mother had forbade him to do.

"Ten, fifteen miles?" I asked, somewhat doubtful.

"Yes, four hours, walking at top speed. And anyway, I got there and my mom freaked out and I climbed up a tree. I refused to come down . . . I was just really driven from a young age."

Bob Knight, the legendary college basketball coach, sees a lot of kids with drive but it's the ones who put in the hard work who succeed. Around the time Bob was promoting his latest book, *The Power of Negative Thinking*, he said to me, "I would tell the parent and the kids that I will be the most demanding coach that you can play for. And if this is going to be a problem for you, you shouldn't even think about coming with us because among other things, you're going to attend every class every day, you're going to be punctual, you're going to have to be on time. You've been a good high school player but you've got a long way really to be a very big college player and that's what we're going to do to develop you . . . I will be very demanding in the class-room and on the basketball floor; in fact, [you] will not have encountered anybody at this point as demanding as I am."

It all goes back to one of the micro-scripts that Graham talked about: "There's just no substitute for hard work."

It got me thinking about what Coach Knight would say about working hard. How would he get *you* to believe in your brand and test you out? What if Coach Knight was your ultimate life coach? I asked him to give me a few pointers.

"The most important thing is this is going to be tougher than you really think it's going to be," he said. "You're a nice looking gal, smart, but I'm going to knock you down a bit, see how you react to it. Are you going to be able to accomplish what I want? If you can't, you won't last very long. Do you realize what it's going to be like when you're here competing with everybody that probably has as good an educational background as you? Smart as you? In the business world, that's what it's all about. What I expect from you—*A, B, C*—if you're not going to be able to do that, deliver in that regard, then you're not going to win."

Learn the *A-B-C* and do the *A-B-M*.

Chapter 2

Why the *Q* Factor Is So Important

How many times has this happened? You hear about a friend who fits a job opening perfectly. She's smart, graduated from all the right schools, attractive, friendly—basically, she has the right pedigree for the position. And yet you find out that surprisingly, she was rejected. It just doesn't seem to make sense.

What if that person were you? How many times have you wondered what happened?

You might, if you understand the *Q* factor.

In television, the Q score is a term to describe what a general audience thinks of a personality, a show, a brand. Does this news anchor have a strong connection with the audience? Is this television show well liked? Do viewers feel good when they see a certain character pop up on the screen? Companies use the *Q* score to determine where they want to advertise and what brands they want to advertise.

Sometimes, a show with a lot of viewers doesn't make a good platform to an advertiser if many viewers actually don't like the content. They're watching because the show is controversial or disturbing and has an addictive quality to it but it doesn't generate a good feeling. In other words, it's not very likable.

Mitt Romney was the perfect president. He had all the right qualifications.

Good education: *check*.

Prior public office experience: *check*.

Smart: *check*.

Strong ideas and business experience: *check*.

No drugs, affairs, seedy skeletons in the closet: *check, check, check* (for God's sake, he drank chocolate milk the morning after his election defeat).

The one thing Mitt Romney didn't have was a high Q score.

I'm not sure if anyone actually measured his Q score but you didn't need to. Everyone I met, Republicans and Democrats alike, said the same thing in the months leading up to the November elections in 2012: Mitt just wasn't likable enough. He was likable to a certain group of people, but to appeal to a country of over 200 million eligible voters, he had to do better. And even though there was a certain group of people who very much did *not* like President Barack Obama, he was likable enough to win the vote.

Don't mistake being likable to being nice. I know some people who are likable by being rather ornery. They're "Mean Joe" Greene on the football field, indomitable and unforgiving. In those instances, it's not because they're ornery, but because they're being genuine: likability is about being genuine and honest.

One of the most enlightening things I read one time went something like this: *people like working with people they like.*

How simple is that? You spend eight-plus hours with your colleagues—you better hope that when you peer up from your computer, you actually feel pleased looking at the people sitting next to you, similarly staring at their computers.

The hard truth is that bosses tend to keep the people around them that they like, even if those people may not be the best at their jobs. The flip side is if *you* are the rather mediocre worker, but a lovable person all around, you'll likely keep your job longer. Likability is a very strong feeling—it's the step before love, and while very few of you will ever love your colleagues, liking them very much leads to great mental satisfaction.

"Being affable and getting along with people is so incredibly important," said Bruce Ratner, the founder of one of the biggest property developers in New York. On the day we met, he'd just signed an agreement to host The MTV Video Music Awards at his arena, The Barclays Center, in Brooklyn. Jay Z and Justin Timberlake were set to perform later in the year. Miley Cyrus would soon make her own distinct splash on the Barclays stage. "You really get rewarded for affability. I've had people work for me who are not that hardworking, people who I don't think are great but they are so affable. People recognize that this is what I call a 'glue' person. They hold things together. Everybody likes them, they're always there for them. If anyone's got a problem, they go into their office to talk about it to them and they do a nice job. Are they *A* people? Not necessarily. They might be *B*."

In some instances, you can be an unlikable person and your boss will still want you around. That's because you're likely a star player. But even that may have an expiration date if your undesirability begins to negate whatever it is you are adding to a company.

Take John Chambers, the CEO of Cisco, one of the largest tech companies. Without getting technical, it manufactures the hidden hardware that connects the world. You might recognize Cisco best from the conference call phone machines they make for offices. We have them at Bloomberg.

John has been one of the longest-serving CEOs in America. He's led Cisco since 1995, some say with an iron fist. But he's also Everyman-ish and like a humble Southern gentleman, John always says "thank you" very emphatically every time we interview on air. During commercial breaks, he likes to chat up a storm about how much he loves being on with me. I know it's part of the game of developing an interview/interviewee rapport, but there's also a certain genuine charm to it. John is a likable guy.

John admitted that in his 18 years of running Cisco, one of the errors he made is tolerating people's misbehaviors because they were such great successes.

"One of the mistakes I made is [keeping] passive-aggressive people in corporations who look after themselves and their own organization first," he said. "I used to think you could modify their behavior, which is true if you stayed on top of them, but the minute they get stress on them or you're not watching, they go back to being that way. In today's world, passive-aggressive behavior is unacceptable at Cisco, and we let them go even though they're a seven-foot tall basketball player who can really shoot baskets."

"Are you able to spot those kinds of people quicker in your company?" I asked.

"Well, I could spot them quicker before, I just thought I could change their behavior. I was a little bit naïve [*laughter*]. And it worked as long as I was watching them!"

The problem is you can't like everybody. And everybody can't like you. It doesn't make you a good or bad person. It just makes you a person.

Women have a harder time with this, period. At least, I can say anecdotally, *I* have had a hard time with this.

Like Sally Field clutching the Oscar to her chest, I just want to know that people like me, they *really, really* do like me.

Except I also know that some people likely hate me. And on any given day, I likely encounter people physically and across the airwaves who hate, love, find me irritating, find me genius, attracted, unattracted, laugh, smile, sneer, resent, admire me. But I also know genuinely I'm a likable person and whatever fleeting feelings are felt, the core is there (see the first chapter for "the company of one").

Sallie Krawcheck, once one of the most senior people on Wall Street, is also very likable. But she's easy not to like. She's successful, beautiful, thin, rich, funny, looks amazing in clothes, and on and on. As Julia Roberts' character said of a beautiful, elegant crème brûlée in *My Best Friend's Wedding*, "it's so irritatingly perfect." Or in reality, it's like the Heidi/Howard Harvard Business School experiment that's now been made famous by Sheryl Sandberg in her bestselling book, *Lean In*, where researchers found that simply switching the gender of a person elicited different feelings from respondents. Overall, Howard was more likable than Heidi even though both possessed the same credentials.

The results of that case study also confirmed something called *confirmation bias*. Sallie recounted a story to me that illustrated this well.

"Years ago, and I'm talking 1998, I reached a point in my career where I thought how in the world do I *not* know the other senior women on Wall Street? This is ridiculous, right?" she said over coffee one day. "So I called a few of them and said, 'I know of you. I want to come over and introduce myself.' Everybody said, yes, that was great.

"I remember one meeting with a very senior woman at Morgan Stanley. I had never seen a picture of her before and I had a visual image of her as I was going to meet with her, in which she was probably six-and-a-half feet tall, probably 275 pounds. And for whatever reason I envisioned her with real gray hair in a bun and granny glasses. A thoroughly horrifying portrait.

"Well, I show up. She was five-foot-two, 104 pounds, beautiful outfit, beautiful hair, beautiful in every way, delightful to be with. Funny. Charming. And we had a wonderful time. And as I was going to leave I said, 'I just have to tell you, but I'm embarrassed to admit it.' And I relayed to her the mental image. So she laughed and she said, 'That's what I thought about you, too.'"

Don't be Selfish: Let Your Voice be Heard

Lou D'Ambrosio is the former CEO of Sears Holdings and someone I got to know through my personal network.

What was the connection? We went to the same high school.

I'd heard early on that Lou graduated from Central High and he had a special affinity for anyone who went to the same school. So I cold e-mailed Lou and told him about our mutual past. Almost immediately I received a warm e-mail and an encouraging note that he would, when the time was right, do an interview with me.

A few months passed and he was finally ready. We got the first television interview with Lou. He walked us through their flagship Sears store near the corporate headquarters in Illinois, discussing the different ways he was attempting to refresh the 120-year-old department store chain.

Lou and I kept in contact after, not just professionally but also as friends. So it was natural that one day while having a pasta lunch in midtown Manhattan, I asked Lou for his best career advice.

Immediately he said the most selfish thing anyone does at a company is hold back their views. That surprised me. Many people hold back their views because they are afraid to speak up, think their views are not worth mentioning, or that the views will get them in trouble. But Lou saw it differently.

"One thing I like to tell my teammates is we need your voice to be heard. A great idea not persuasively communicated just does not count. If you have an idea and you are not persuasively communicating it, in many ways it's selfish, it's unfair. Now, how you communicate it is just as important as what you communicate. And I think showing some humility when you communicate, exposing some of your vulnerabilities when you communicate, is endearing."

"Like saying, 'I don't know a lot about this, but . . . ?'" I asked.

"Yes, something like, 'This may not be a great idea but what do you think about this?' Or to say, 'You know, I respect what others have said, but I just don't agree with it' . . . because I'm telling you, there are people with great ideas who do not communicate them well and who don't get credit for it. And people with pretty good ideas who are wonderful communicators probably get more credit than they deserve."

The downside, Lou said, about encouraging people to express their views is that everybody ends up wanting to meet with him. He said he instituted the "Power of 10" rule which was if an idea couldn't be told in 10 minutes or 10 slides, then it wasn't worth his time.

And for those who seek him out to just talk about themselves? "Sometimes I hide from them," he joked.

Some people would say Sallie actually had two knocks against her when it came to likability. Not only was she a powerful business-woman, but she worked in an industry that's notoriously unlikable. Remember Occupy Wall Street and the throngs of protesters in 2011 and 2012 marching the streets against those "fat cat bankers?"

So it is a little strange that one of the inspirations for this chapter came from a longtime Wall Street banker named James "Jimmy" B. Lee Jr., who works right alongside Jamie Dimon at JPMorgan as Vice Chairman. Jimmy is a legend in the banking world, having helped create and finance some of the biggest deals over the last 30 years. Rupert Murdoch credits Jimmy for his deal to buy Dow Jones and during the financial crisis, Jimmy was right at the center of the bailouts of Chrysler, GM, and AIG. In 2013, he helped founder Michael Dell take his computer company private.

Jimmy and I met when he first came into our Bloomberg studios to do an interview on the passing of his good friend, Teddy Forstmann. True to his reputation, Jimmy was funny and self-deprecating, which you wouldn't expect from a "Wall Street guy." When we talked again a few months later, I asked him how he's been able to have such a long career in banking when so many others eventually crash and burn. He replied that part of it was understanding how to connect to people, tapping into your "EQ."

"I think you can run an enterprise for a while and not be liked," he said. "But I don't think you can run an enterprise over the long term and not be liked. Short term, a dictator can get results. Long term, one day he or she will lead the troops up the hill and someone will shoot him or her in the back.

"What makes Jamie so special is he has the best IQ, EQ, and Q," he continued. "In fact, he is more than likable. Even if we never met each other in business, we would still be great friends."

What does confirmation bias have to do with likability?

We like and dislike things, people, and places based on our own confirmation biases. If a person likes gun control, there's a pretty good chance that person is not going to like a firearm-bearing farmer from Texas. Every time you pick up the phone to call your local cable com-pany, you're pretty certain you'll dislike the experience, based on your past experiences and hearing about other people's past experiences. Even if you have one or two great encounters with the most gracious cable company operator in the world, you'll still hold the view that cable companies know diddly-squat about customer service. I once live-messaged Netflix about my service and was taken aback by how cheerful and enthusiastic "Nathalie" was on the other line, ending all her sentences with "!" or sometimes "!!!" I felt how much Netflix wanted me to like them and saw them as different from those annoying cable television companies.

We tend to hold these confirmation biases until we're proven wrong consistently. Unfortunately there are times when our first impressions are the only ones. Take for example what I said in the beginning of this chapter about the perfect candidate for the job. For one reason or another, the interviewer did not like this person and did not select her for the job. Maybe it was the fact that she was too perfect. Maybe she didn't seem genuine in her answers. Maybe the interviewer just simply didn't *like* her and for whatever reason, that can happen. Whatever the case, there isn't another chance to prove the confirmation bias wrong.

Likability is partly based on proving these confirmation biases wrong. It helps to be a genuinely nice and giving person, but likability is about doing things that nobody would expect. It's about being genuine when others are fake, giving when others are selfish, calm when others are panicking. And doing it from a good place deep inside your heart. I'm not saying likability is all about this. In fact, a large part of likability is just innate—some people are, for certain reasons, more likable than others. But it is one part of likability that you have some control over.

Mitt Romney was well on his way to being more likable when he outperformed President Barack Obama in the first presidential debate. Here was a candidate who people saw as yet another rich, privileged, white man and people were ready to hear more snobby comments about how much smarter he was than the rest of us. Instead, he appeared humbled, caring, and genuinely passionate about improving the lives of Americans.

Then, as we all know, the *Mother Jones* underground video hit the web and it all but affirmed voters' confirmation bias. He really was just another rich, privileged, white man who thought he was smarter and better than 47 percent of us. In a matter of a morning news cycle, Mitt Romney became less likable.

When Sallie Krawcheck was fired from Bank of America, she could have retired from the public eye and lived off her millions.

Instead, she spoke out about being fired. She admitted how tough and embarrassing it was. She said she was *grateful* for being fired because it made her stronger. And in that moment, she became more likable to all the people who thought she was just another cold, steely woman crushing people on the way up the ladder of Wall Street.

Back in 1936, Dale Carnegie wrote the classic book *How to Win Friends and Influence People.* In the ensuing years, there have been hundreds of management and advice books of the same ilk, teaching people how to be more liked. From what I can tell and observe, there are really just a few basic things to keep in mind. They may not make you instant friends, but they do go a long way in making you more likable.

Put others ahead of you: This comes from Dave Kerpen, the CEO of Likeable Media, who helps companies develop a more "likable" culture. "The number one way to be more likable—above all things—is to put others first. Look for how you can be of value before your own personal or professional gain," he said. "It seems completely counterintuitive to some but it absolutely works. The most important words you can say at any meeting are, 'How can I help you?' So many people are out for themselves, when you go out of your way to help someone else, you're going to be more likable."

Follow up: Sounds simple, right? You'd be surprised how many people say they'll do this or that and never follow up. I've committed this crime many times, and every time I've done it, I regretted it tremendously. The times I do stay on and follow up I've been rewarded. Following up is an extension of keeping your word. When you say you'll follow up with an e-mail, do it. When you say you'll follow up in two weeks with a call, do it. When you don't, it's tough to regain any credibility.

Be consistently timely: While celebrities and presidents may be notoriously tardy, *you* can't. Being consistently late is a sign that you don't care about the other person's time. I appreciate when my guests—no matter how important they are—arrive early or just on time for their segments. I was once late to a lunch with a Wall Street CEO and the next time we met for lunch, he made sure that I was sitting at the table before he walked over from the office. It was a sharp message: Please don't keep people waiting or you might be in the same boat. "Traffic" is a get-out-of-jail free card you can only use once with someone.

Say something genuine: Every parent can identify with this. Your child brings home a painting or an essay and you want to love it, but frankly, it's just not that great. Instead of lying and saying how beautiful the drawing is, pick out something genuinely nice about it. Like the bold use of colors or the shapes of the clouds.

This works with adults too. If you want to make someone feel good, pick out one thing that genuinely stands out. It can be whatever: the way a scarf looks; the color of their hair; how they park the car, as long as it's genuine.

In the workplace, if you're going to compliment someone, don't just say, "This is great!" or "What an amazing job you're doing!" I can't tell you how many times people have come up to me and said, "I love your show!" when I know they haven't even watched it. It's the people who say, "I really liked the guest you had the other day" or "I liked the segment you guys did on Google" who make me feel their compliments are genuine. I try to do the same myself. After a lunch with someone, I don't say, "Thank you for the lunch, you are really great." I pick out something. "What you said about X really struck a chord." It goes a long way in making you connect with someone. You're paying attention and you're being genuine.

Chapter 3

How to Network

There are few scenarios at work that I dread more than having to go to a cocktail party to network. It's all part of the job but there is nothing natural about walking around to groups of people you don't know with dorky looking Office Depot nametags hanging off your lapel.

I asked Harry Wilson, the private equity partner turned political candidate turned bankruptcy expert, how he does it. "First thing I do is go to the bar. Usually people there are lining up and getting drinks and that's easiest to meet people," he said. "Most people are likable and like to talk and it's easy to strike up a conversation. I did that a few weeks ago—I didn't know anyone at this function so I went up to get coffee— I don't drink coffee—and struck up a conversation with the guy next to me. Turns out we knew some people in common and from there, I met more people."

I had a chance a few weeks later to experiment with Harry's method. I was invited to a cocktail event held at a bank's headquarters and hundreds of people were gathered. I knew I'd know some people but I wouldn't exactly consider them friends. After a quick hello to the host who was like the father at a wedding reception, greeting well-dressed people as they emerged from designated elevators, I briskly walked towards the bar and ordered a glass of wine. At that moment, another man—an older gentleman—was also ordering a drink so I struck up a conversation. Turns out he was with Traveler's Insurance and frankly, we had very little to discuss. After a few minutes, I was ready to meet someone else.

Just to the right of me were two gentlemen deep in conversation. High school panic swept over me for a moment as I realized I didn't want to look like the lonely girl at a party, so I popped my head into their speaking mid-sentence and said, "Sorry to interrupt . . . " I boldly stuck my hand out. They were very nice and one of the men, who spoke in an Italian accent, said his business was based in New Jersey. Okay, so it wasn't exactly a strong connection, but at least I could conjure up a few points about the state where I live.

Luckily, I am not the only one in these shoes. A few minutes later, another middle-aged man in a three-piece suit walked up to the three of us and introduced himself. He worked for the bank and recognized me from television. We all talked about that for a little while but the conversation was rapidly fading away when I heard "Betty!"

It was my old editor from the *Financial Times*. Bingo—a familiar face! Robert Thomson walked over with his big, friendly smile and while I said "So great to see you here!" what I really wanted to say was, "Thank God, I've never been happier to see you here because I'm feeling really awkward by myself." We talked for a little while and caught up on old times until the bell rang which meant everyone needed to be herded into the dining room like docile sheep. But at least I got through my cocktail party without too much of a sweat.

Maybe you're one of the rare individuals who have never experienced this. In that case, you're one of two things: a very famous person or a person who travels constantly with a companion. For the rest of the working population, this is just another element of office life.

Networking is not just about cocktail parties, of course. Networking is essentially doing something that connects you with another person for the benefit of hopefully, both your careers. I've met people who are constantly networking, whether they're at a baseball game, at the office or at a party. The world is a playground of new people to meet and new connections to make and the more people they meet, the more energy they have. These are extroverted people and tend to be looked upon as successful and lucky people. And why wouldn't they be if they're always meeting new people and making new connections.

Other people network by using the Internet and by that, I mean LinkedIn. I've tried to resist mentioning this company too much for fear of looking like a commercial for them but the truth is, almost every single CEO or executive I've talked to mentioned LinkedIn as a place where they look up potential hires or to connect with someone else.

Dan Portillo is the talent partner at Greylock Partners, one of the most successful venture capital firms, whose investments include Facebook, Pandora, and . . . LinkedIn. His job is basically meeting people all day and figuring out where they fit best in the dozens of companies his firm invests in. He networks constantly.

"Of all the social media sites, by far LinkedIn is the most valuable," he told me, acknowledging he is an investor. "I use it every day, my team uses it every day, for a variety of reasons. I use LinkedIn several times a day, I always have it open and I use it to find people, often do background checks in conjunction with meetings. When I have a meeting, I'll ask my assistant to put in a LinkedIn profile in the meeting request. I want to know who do we know in common. I get a better sense of the individual and people who are connected really strong to me are probably good to network with.

"A number of people got hired after reaching out to me on LinkedIn. I tell people who are graduating school to use LinkedIn by finding profiles of people they are interested in meeting, what types of jobs they have that they would want, getting a list of what those people look like, and approaching them."

Interviewing for a Job: How to Pass the Taste Test

Teresa Taylor is the former chief operating officer of Qwest, a big telecom company. When she came to visit our Bloomberg studios to discuss her book *The Balance Myth: Rethinking Work–Life Success*, she struck me as pretty no nonsense and humble. Her sister-in-law came with her to the interview. She patiently waited around to grab a conference room, e-mailing until I was finished with my radio program. I noticed her relaxed demeanor, which I took to be because she was free of the stresses of corporate life.

She ran a company with 30,000 employees and she was one of the most senior women in a male-dominated industry. Her rise to the top, she said, had a lot to do with her ability to make decisions quickly. She looked for that trait in people she hired, which got us onto the topic of interviewing people for jobs.

"My trick to interviewing is to have a meal with somebody. When you go to dinner or lunch or breakfast with somebody, you see the true person. And here's my example. Just getting there, you know, can they? I mean, this sounds silly, but can we walk, and talk, and sit down? Are they polite to the wait staff? Can they even order off the menu? If I was with one of those people who sits down, 'Oh, you know, can I have this but not that? And this, but not that?'. . . Have you ever had a friend like that?"

"Yes," I answer.

"For goodness sakes, just order! To me, that was a deal breaker. Because they can't even look at a menu and make a decision. You know, let's just get on with it. So I've had people I thought I was going to hire, after having a meal, I've reversed it."

"Was there one interview question you'd always ask?" I said.

"You know, probably the open-ended one. 'Can you give me two things' of whatever. If they couldn't stay focused on answering with two . . . it's amazing how many people will not even give you two clear answers. They blab on and on. Again, it was that decision-making processing. Could this person be a leader?"

Unlike Dan, I find lunches to be *my* most effective networking tool. I go into every lunch with the goal of three things:

1. A further connection with my lunch companion.
2. Story and guest ideas.
3. The introduction to new people.

I try to always send a follow-up thank-you e-mail the next day.

Why do lunches work for me? When I first started in the Hong Kong bureau of Dow Jones Newswires, my bureau chief said there was one thing he learned from Marcus Brauchli that stuck with him. Marcus is now the vice president of The Washington Post Company, but in those days, Marcus was working in Asia for the *Wall Street Journal*. My bureau chief said that what he observed was every day, no matter what, Marcus always made sure to have a lunch scheduled. It didn't matter if the source he was meeting had a potential story or not, but he made sure he was always out of the office at lunch every single day meeting people. To me, that was why Marcus Brauchli was where he was.

What stuck with my bureau chief, stuck with me.

As I mentioned earlier, about the time I was doing my research for this book, Sheryl Sandberg's book, *Lean In*, was published. Among the difficulties Sheryl described women encountered at work was networking. How do women find the right mentors to help them move up the rank?

Sandberg very appropriately described how the undertone of sex made it sometimes difficult for women to seek older men as mentors (a big problem when the majority of senior managers will undoubtedly be an older man). Harvey Golub, who ran American Express for eight years mostly in the 1990s, agreed with Sandberg.

"I've treated [men and women] both fairly but there are things I would not do with a woman employee that I would do with a male," he recalled. "I would not go to a lunch with a woman employee alone. I would not have a woman employee in my office with the door closed. If I had a woman in my office, I'd tell my secretary to not leave her station. I wouldn't go to cocktails with a woman alone . . . and part of the reason is I have seen a very large number of made-up sexual harassment suits and so I wouldn't do those things. Now, it never would have prevented me from promoting a woman. I mean, that's my attitude."

Sandberg advocated for more formal mentoring networks and highlighted a study that suggested women did better professionally when they joined formal networks than when they tried informal networking such as what I described above with my lunches.

That part of the book was perhaps the one that stood out to me the most. Not because there was any new information but because Sandberg hit upon what I believe is one of the biggest reasons why women drop out of the workforce. While much of the debate in America is about how women can work and have children at the same time, not enough centers on why women aren't able to network properly. And when they can't, they unfortunately get left behind.

What does left behind look like?

According to the Center for Work–Life Policy, more than half of all new hires in the United States—53 percent—are women.

By the time they're promoted to vice president, only 26 percent are women.

At the executive committee level, just 14 percent.

Women CEOs at Fortune 500 companies? About 3 percent.

So is networking the reason why women get left behind? A McKinsey study in 2011 found that family and children are *not* the biggest reasons women drop out of the workforce or leave for another company. It might be, unfortunately, the perfect face-saving excuse.

What holds women back, according to McKinsey researchers, are

1. A lack of access to informal networks and mentors.
2. An imbedded mind-set that women can't handle tougher—and therefore, more senior—jobs.

While it's tough to quantify or identify who has this mind-set, we all know it's there. Even *you* may have this mind-set.

I point this out because networking is not something you ought to do, it's something you *need* to do if you want to advance your career. But if you think just because you can't golf or "hang with the guys" at the cigar bar you are at a severe disadvantage, you're wrong. There are so many other ways to network and, if you make it your priority, you'll make the connections.

CEOs and Their Mentors

Many of the CEOs I talked to, when asked about networking, almost always named their mentors. Every single one of them had a mentor that changed their lives and, not surprisingly, the first one would almost always be a parent.

"I was fascinated by investing at a very young age," Warren Buffett said. "I got it by going down to my Dad's office on

Saturdays when I was seven or eight and they had these books around and I would start reading them. When I finished reading those, I went to the public library and read them all. But why I did that, nobody told me to . . . my Dad was not that fascinated. He just thought it was kind of amusing that I was. He always encouraged me in everything I did, but he did not push me at all into what I ended up doing."

"My mother would sit down with us at six years old and she would take the *Reader's Digest* which had vocabulary words in it and she would go over the vocabulary words. My mother was very involved in our education," Bruce Ratner, the prominent New York real estate developer, recounted. "My father would always look at my report card. I don't think my father knew what grade I was in, he really didn't . . . but he had a very heavy Yiddish Jewish accent. When I went to elementary school, I was the only kid whose father had an accent. When I grew up, it was different in New York. So he wouldn't come to class often, I think he was embarrassed. So he used to say, he'd look at my report card and he would say, 'Ruski—he used to call me Ruski—Ruski, you get a quarter. A quarter for an *A*, nothing for a *B*.' That's it—a quarter for an *A* and nothing for a *B*."

Beyond the initial influence of parents, almost everyone had one or two mentors who said and did things that affected their careers permanently. As mentioned before, a big misconception is you need an army of mentors to help your career—in fact, it's almost always the case that you'll deeply connect with only a handful of individuals. The size of their impact will far surpass their puny numbers.

After talking about his parents, Bruce went on to describe another major influence in his life, the former New York Mayor Ed Koch.

"I model myself a lot on him," Bruce said. "I try to be like Ed Koch. I try to be outgoing. I try to be direct, honest with people in conversation. I try not to be afraid to take difficult positions. I often say to myself, 'How would Ed do this?'"

Sallie Krawcheck reminisces about her first sponsor who was "a fellow by the name of Westin Hicks. He was a research analyst covering property and casualty insurance for Sanford Bernstein. He took an interest in me. We talked to each other. We had offices next to each other and this was when I was a life insurance analyst. So we're talking Stone Ages. We probably talked to each other twenty or thirty times a day. In the first instance, he's saying, 'Let me read your research. Okay, you know be careful about this, I made this mistake when I was younger. Watch this.' And then after a long, long time, I was doing the same for him. It was a good back and forth, two-way, deep relationship. If you have to ask somebody [to be a sponsor], you're done. The sponsor or mentor needs to get a lot out of it, and maybe not as much out of it as you do; but it's not a one-way street."

For Ralph Schlosstein, the CEO of boutique investment bank, Evercore Partners, sometimes all it takes is a few choice words from a senior official to influence your life. He recalled his beginning as a 20-something college graduate working in Washington. He was listening to a lecture given by a staff director of the Joint Economic Committee, John Stark, that was pretty standard.

"At the conclusion of this discussion, he said, 'You know, if you remember one sentence from this entire discussion, remember this one. That the people that you step on on your way up the ladder will be there to kick you on your way down.' That was probably the best thing that was ever said to me and it was said to me by my very first boss at my very first meeting with him."

This saying made a similar impact on Bob Benmosche, the CEO of the bailed-out insurance company AIG, but it came out of his mother's mouth when she described the sorry fate of one of his uncles.

"She was very sad because this guy, people kissed his ass on the way up and they're stepping on his shirt on the way down," he told me. "And so: Stay realistic, understand your place, don't become too important and you'll be fine. And when people are not, it annoys the hell out of me."

Formal networks can sometimes be effective because at least everyone is going in with a singular purpose. If you're going into the cheese shop, you're getting cheese; you're not getting a pound of salmon. Okay?

But sometimes informal is the most effective way to network. Anne Mulcahy, the former CEO of Xerox, doesn't buy the "old boys' network" as the barrier to success. She says the problem is some people, especially women, don't know how to network or find mentors naturally.

"It has to be done in the context of work. It has to be done, I think, in a very seamless way and I think sometimes we put these arbitrary mentoring programs in and we point to the powerful and say that person is important in your career," she said. "And then we look inauthentic and overly ambitious versus what I think is much more important, which is in the context of your work, certainly to manage up well but not to do it exclusive of managing or building relationships with your peers and the people who work for you as being equally important.

"I've watched women derail their careers because they're not good at [networking]," she said. "They work really hard at it, they put so much emphasis on this kind of 'managing up' thing that they're not well liked, they don't have great relationships with their peers. . . . I don't want to talk about *Lean In* because I think it's a great book, and of course it's inspiring, but there are some women who spend all their time leaning in and what I'm worried about is just that people get the wrong message that they have to lean in all the time. I thought Sheryl's book did address the nuances—you have to be genuine, you have to be humble, you have to be likable. But for a lot of women who may have not read the book, they just hear about it, they might think, 'Oh my God, I've got to just be aggressive all the time.'"

Let me pause for a moment here to emphasize Anne's point because I think it's a great one. Women have a complicated relationship with being humble. Already viewed as the weaker sex, it's difficult for some women, as they rise up the ranks professionally, to show humility for fear of looking vulnerable. Or the opposite happens—women put their skills or contributions down so much that they really do come across as insecure or incapable.

When I was just starting out in my career, I heard a woman speaker advise all the women in the audience never to start an e-mail with "I'm sorry but . . ." or "I hope . . ." She said it made women look weak and hesitant. She was so firm about this that I put it to practical use until I quickly realized for some people, the soft and humble approach works better . . . like with other women.

The key is knowing when and how to use the power of humility. Most humble people are actually quite self-confident—they have a strong core that allows them to downplay themselves to get their point across. When I lived in Atlanta, the number of Southerners who rose to the Oval Office was pointed out to me: Jimmy Carter, Bill Clinton, two George Bushes. Southern charm was also a humble charm—Southerners downplayed their success so that you would like them more. Sallie Krawcheck, the Wall Street investment banker, hails from South Carolina and she possesses that strong but humble personality. She never misses a moment to poke fun at herself but you know deep down, it would take a hurricane to really rattle her nerves. Nowadays, I start off a lot of e-mails—not all, mind you—with "I'm sorry to bother you . . ." or "I hope you don't mind . . ." and not once do I ever feel those e-mails are ignored.

All of which got me thinking, to tell someone networking is important is one thing but what about actually doing it? When experts say that naturalness has to be a part of networking, what does that mean? When I first started in television, all my talent coaches kept telling me, "Be natural! Be natural!" on camera, which was probably the worst advice to give someone just starting out. If you have to be told to be natural, you most definitely don't know how to do it.

The thing that helped me may be what helps someone when it comes to networking—know, at the very least, what *not* to do.

Know, as Anne points out above, *not to be too aggressive*. And by aggressive, the meaning is two-fold: one is physical aggression (frequent e-mails or phone calls) and the second is tone. I can't count the number of CEOs and senior executives who told me what a turnoff it was to have people stop by their offices with a "What can you do for me?" attitude.

On the flip side, groveling often is also aggressive. People usually like to help, but if the people they're helping come across as too thankful, it can be a turnoff. Remember that networking is also about what *you* bring to the table. Never devalue what you can bring to a relationship, even if you're junior and the mentor is very senior. You're seeking help but you're not looking to be rescued.

Which brings me to this: know *not to be so helpless*. I can attest to this because it sometimes happens to me: A young person will arrive with many questions about his or her future and expect you (the senior person) to presumably make their entire life decision in a matter of minutes. It's very unnatural and very dangerous. Instead of asking, "What should I do?" ask "What would *you* do?" Instead of asking someone to give advice about your future, ask the person about their background, how they got to where they were, what shaped their outlook. It's a much better way to make a connection, you learn much more, and you form the basis of a future relationship.

Not everyone you meet will connect with you. Many people you network with will be occasional contacts and it's important to maintain the relationships. But real mentoring happens with only a few individuals. I can count on one hand the number of people I really can say are true mentors. Many of the CEOs I interviewed mentioned their parents as the biggest and first mentors in their lives. Having a big Rolodex is important but when it comes to mentoring, quality versus quantity is most important.

Know also *not to be so fussy*. Fussiness is divisive—it's negative, boring, and distracting. By fussy I mean fussy with your hair, your food, your attitude, talking too much, just overall tense. People want to be relaxed around others—the golf course is a perfect place to network because there's nothing more relaxing than standing on the pastoral green under a big blue sky in your lemon drop-colored polo shirt. Even Quasimodo would look like your best friend in that setting.

One well-known newscaster, when I asked him how he gets all the big interviews, said he doesn't always pressure the guests for an interview. Sometimes he calls them up just to say hello and to talk about everything else except for what he'd really like to discuss which is, "Please come on the program." People want to network naturally and not feel they are always "on" for business. That's a big lesson I've been learning myself and getting much better at. The more you can connect on a personal level, the deeper and more meaningful the relationship.

Know *not to think of yourself so much*. This is rich coming from someone on television. But the reality is to successfully network—to really be able to find that connection with someone—you have to think of what you can do for that person first. Sound familiar? It's also the way to become more likable. If you just think of these six words—"What can I do to help?"—you can change your relationships with the people around you and find a deeper connection.

On this topic, I turned to Adam Grant, a professor at the Wharton School at my alma mater, the University of Pennsylvania. Before March 2013, not many people knew about Adam. But after a *New York Times Magazine* piece profiled his research and book, *Give and Take*, he became a much sought-after voice on leadership and success. His research primarily focused on the power of giving. The title of the piece said it all: "Is Giving the Secret to Getting Ahead?"

Adam's way of networking is to keep giving—giving his time, resources, energy away to anyone who sought his help. His inbox was loaded with hundreds of e-mails from people seeking help or advice every day. He mentioned in the piece that he rarely turned anyone away. The author of the article seemed exhausted by Adam's constant altruism.

I decided I would contact him and see for myself. One Sunday, I e-mailed him a request for comment at 11:51 A.M. At 11:52, I received:

Hi Betty,

It's wonderful to hear from you. I love your program, and greatly appreciated your coverage of my LinkedIn post on negotiations a few weeks ago.

I'm delighted to hear that you're writing a book, and I'll be honored to answer the questions below. More soon. . . .

Cheers,
Adam

Sure enough, by 8 P.M., I had a thoughtful, lengthy e-mail on why giving was very helpful to networking. He wrote:

1. When it comes to networking, people "give" by sharing their knowledge and connections with the people they meet. Giving is crucial to networking; it creates a deeper and wider web of connections, granting us the goodwill and access that allow us to find jobs and excel in those jobs. Most of us give to our strong ties—the people we know well and trust, but evidence shows that this limits our access to novel ideas, as our strongest ties tend to share redundant information: They know many of the same people and much of the same information that we do. There are two other groups of ties who offer more efficient access to new information and opportunities: weak ties and dormant ties. Weak ties are acquaintances, and dormant ties are the people we used to know. Since these two groups travel in different circles and are exposed to diverse ideas, they're invaluable sources of knowledge and connections. For example, one study by David Obstfeld showed that the employees who played the most central roles in innovation were those who regularly introduced colleagues who could benefit from knowing each other. Similarly, Jim Berry and I found that the most creative employees in multiple organizations were those who not only took an interest in their work, but also went out of their way to contribute to others.

2. The biggest mistake people make when they give to others in a work context is self-sacrificing. It's impossible to help all of the people all of the time with all of the requests, and people who try to say yes to everything put themselves at risk for burning out and being exploited. I find that the key to effective giving is setting boundaries on who, how, and when you help. By setting clear priorities about which groups to help, specializing in particular kinds of helping, and blocking out time for individual tasks, people can help others and achieve success at the same time.

To sum up, Adam advises: Expand your giving to people you don't know well or used to know and be selective at times so you don't burn out. Sound advice from the professor.

And in the process, I made a new connection.

From the Recruiting Side: The Rule of 100

Dan Portillo, the venture capital talent executive, has a high-class problem. He works with companies that are growing so fast they are running into an issue: How do I get as many people as I can to work for me and how do I make sure they are the best? It's a difficult lesson for tech entrepreneurs-turned-CEOs to realize that while they may be innovators, they can be terrible employers. That's where Dan comes in. He works with hiring managers to find top talent. While the problem may seem small, it's quite remarkable how a few bad apples in an organization can nearly destroy a corporate culture. I heard this from Elon Musk, John Chambers, Jamie Dimon, and many other CEOs.

In early 2013, Dan put together a slide presentation called "Owning Your Recruiting" that lit up the social media sphere. It showed up on the *Business Insider* website where Dan was quoted as saying: "The only way you can effectively support 50-plus portfolio companies is to help them build phenomenal recruiting engines inside their company."

When I later spoke to Dan he told me about the concept called The 100 Rule.

"I wanted people to know just exactly how much outreach it takes. If you think you're going to e-mail five or ten people and hire someone out of that, it's just not going to happen. So if you look at a response rate somewhere between ten and twenty percent, if you reach out to one hundred people, ten to twenty of those are going to respond and maybe half of them will be open to being hired . . . five to ten qualified people out of that group of one hundred . . . you're lucky to get one person [for the job]. I mostly want to make a point that it requires a huge amount of outreach to actually get to qualified candidates. For some of the people that have been recruiting or are managers for the first time, they're shocked at that number. But I think most people in Silicon Valley are getting used to it."

Chapter 4

Asking for a Raise

When I walk into Chris Burch's office, he's curled up like a cat on his sofa chair.

I've been warned beforehand that this billionaire and ex-husband of fashion designer, Tory Burch, is a little bit eccentric. And true to form, when he sees me enter, he uncurls and springs up with a gigantic smile, all while darting his eyes from my shoes—"How lovely!"—to my gold cuff buttons—"They look just like screw heads"—to my dress—"What a beautiful color."

Chris is the quintessential company of one—he has never worked for anyone in his life because he's a constant entrepreneur. His biggest success was creating the fashion brand that bears his ex-wife's name and now he's out on his own with his C. Wonder retail chain, along with various investments from Powermat (wireless powering), to Liquipel (water repellant), to five-star hotels.

"You ever been to Indonesia? I own a beautiful resort there, just near Bali," he said. "You *must go*. Pink just stayed there. I'll give you a nice price."

I ask him what his biggest career mistake was and what he learned from it.

"Everything, so many things. I invested in codfish. I didn't realize commodities moved that market. I learned you have to invest in something you have *control* over. With cod, the feed costs more than the fish. Whenever I think I'm really smart, I realize I have to be careful . . . when things are the best—sell, when things are the worst—buy!"

The conversation jumps from his childhood learning disabilities to his love of crystals—"not going to start a business in them because most people don't like them"—to why men are so afraid.

"If you want to meet a boy, just repeat what he says because men are so deeply insecure," he advises. "Like he says to you, 'I just had the most amazing vacation in wherever' and you repeated it, he'd say later that you were the most amazing girl he ever met!"

A little bit later: "Give me any product, anything!"

"A bowling ball," I reply.

He slumps down in his chair, snaps his loafers onto the coffee table, and closes his eyes. A thick silence occupies the air. He's about to come up with an instant marketing campaign for bowling balls.

"Hmmmm, oh this is a really good one. Last one I had was spices. Hmm, bowling ball. *New* bowling ball. Two things. One, bowlers have trouble gripping. Make something very simple. Grips that will go on the end of each of your fingers. One of the grips will be a tracking device. Taking the technology from tennis and put it in bowling. We'll have an app that will track your bowling bowl as it goes down the lane. As you're waiting for your next frame, it'll show you that you released it here and here's where it went. Very simple tracking device— either a glove for tracking device in it or a ball with the tracking device in it. Sell it for $2.99, which is what a regular ball costs. We can make it in China for less money. Motto: Why should the pros know more than you?"

He opens his eyes and gives me an expectant look. I respond with "I'm impressed!"

But what really impressed me was a little later when I asked him to answer a simple question.

"What advice would you give someone asking for a raise?"

For the first time, he stares at me in silence, and then scrunches his nose. "What do you *mean*? Do people still really *do* that?"

"Of course they do," I reply. And in a moment we both remark at how disconnected he is from the rest of us, the people who work for a salary.

"It just shows you how flawed I am. I believe so strongly in equity," he says. "People don't understand equity in terms of salary. Most people want salary (and stability) over equity. I've never had to ask for a raise. I've never had to do it. You're right. It's really f***ed up!"

I consider Chris one of the lucky ones. For the rest of us, we all have to do the dreaded ask-for-a-raise dance every year. For a ritual that is so commonplace at work, it's alarming how so few of us know how to do it.

Google the phrase "ask for a raise" and you get 295 million results. Books abound on how to do this. Every executive coach or financial expert has some advice on how to increase your salary.

As Fred Kofman, a frequently quoted expert on coaching and leadership, and a faculty member of *Lean In*, writes: "The only way you can command a better salary is *for you to be more valuable to your employer than anyone else who could do your job* [his emphasis]. And therefore, the only way to raise your salary is to make a higher contribution to your employer than you are making now."

When I first started my reporting career at Dow Jones Newswires, I had no idea how exactly I was adding to the profits of the company. If I was a car salesman, I got it—the more cars I sold, the more I made the dealership and the more valuable I was. But I had a hard time figuring out how my reporting was directly increasing the money made by the company.

One day, I was sitting in my editor's office.

"Congratulations, Betty. We heard from sales that one of your stories convinced a client to subscribe to our service," he said to me. "He thought it was a great piece and it made him realize he needed to have our news service all the time."

Needless to say, I was pleased with myself but more so because I finally had some sliver of understanding that I was adding value to the company. Of course years later I understand the power of content—exclusive content—and the value of what I produce.

At various times, I've committed both the best and worst things to do when you ask for a raise.

One time I'd written down a list of my best, exclusive stories and demanded a 10 percent raise and got it. I knew my editor valued my work and didn't want to see me leave so in matter of weeks, I was 10 percent richer.

Another time I did exactly the same thing at the same company and got nothing. The difference? Another boss. He wasn't as invested in my career as my prior manager.

One time I'd jumped to a new job and nearly doubled my salary. The next time I took the first salary offer because I was so desperate to get the job I was too scared to seem demanding (big mistake, as my boss advised me later).

As I was researching this, I noticed a few common threads in asking for a raise. None of them were very earth shattering because they all boiled down to these pointers:

- Know how much other people in your position are making.
- Give concrete examples of what you've accomplished for the company.
- Don't talk about your personal needs as in, "I need to pay my mortgage."
- Ask for a private meeting in person with the boss.
- Don't threaten to quit.

One thing I noticed in all my reading, though, was that very few people bothered to ask what it was like to be the person who's supplying the raise. In other words, what does your boss really think when you walk into his or her office asking for a raise?

I decided to pose that question to a few CEOs who undoubtedly have been put in that position. Harvey Golub, the former CEO of American Express and former Chairman of AIG, was my first interviewee, mostly because since he was retired, he wouldn't hesitate to give an honest answer.

"First of all, if they're asking for a raise, then they believe there's something in the process that's unfair, and most bosses won't think about [your salary] as unfair," he said. "Let's say there's two different events. One is they got an offer from somebody else, and the question is do they go to their boss and say, 'You know, I got an offer from X company to double my compensation. Would you care to match it?' That's one approach, and people do that.

"Another approach is to go to somebody and I think this is a better one: 'I think I'm being paid less than I should be, given the quality of the work I do, so I would ask you to take a look at that.'"

"That wouldn't cause you to bristle?" I ask.

"No. That's being very respectful of a process."

"What would you find annoying?"

"Oh, if somebody came and said, 'I just got an offer from X company at twice the income.' I would make the decision as it was . . . but I might say, 'Well, that is a big difference, Betty, and that might be a better thing for you.' If you came in and said, 'They're offering twenty-five percent more,' then I might say to you, 'That's interesting. That kind of shows how valuable you are. You need to consider the following things.' But my reaction would be 'I'm going to lose Betty pretty soon, so I better find a replacement for her.'"

"Whereas you would never have thought that initially—that you had to find a replacement."

"Yep. And I would get a backup plan in place."

"Now, what if someone were to say to you, 'I know so-and-so is making this much, and I'm not making as much as that person and I do the same job,' or something along those lines . . . that would not play well with you?" I ask.

"No," he replied. "First of all, you may be wrong. I can't correct you, or if I tried to correct you, you wouldn't believe me." And then he added with a humor in his voice: "It would be unlikely that I could say, 'Well, Betty, Sue really does a *much* better job than *you* [laughter].'

"Now, you could go to somebody and say, 'You know, I thought the raise that I got this year was relatively low. Could you talk me through how you go about the process and what things you consider and how you came to the number you did?'"

"I was just recently advising somebody in the company [who asked for a raise]," replied Sheila Marcelo, the founder of Care.com. "She had a great relationship with me, great relationship with her boss's boss, and she went around and went through somebody else who then went and had a conversation with her boss' boss, and her boss' boss felt like, 'We have a relationship. Why isn't she just having this conversation with me?' And so she went about it in a kind of either lacking trust or lacking confidence kind of way, yet she's asking for a promotion, and she's asking for a raise which was sort of not aligned."

"That's contradictory," I affirmed.

"Yes, so thinking about the process is really important. We've set it up so that people have an understanding and expectation. We have regular performance reviews so that you're not creating an uncomfortable environment to be able to have these conversations," she said. "There's a method to it rather than some random process, because whenever it's random for employees, they think that it's not fair. They think there's favoritism. But if you create sort of an objective process around it, it makes it a lot easier."

And on it went. I came to the conclusion that no matter what, asking for a raise is an unpleasant situation because it puts you at odds with your boss. And moreover, it raises the specter that you may leave (or that the boss may think you want to leave). It's a risk no matter how you slice it.

So no wonder there are so many articles advising how one is to do this and no wonder not many of them are very satisfying. You're walking into a situation where the other person usually holds most of the cards and your only leverage is to leave. More often than not, the talks won't exactly turn out the way you want. But then again, it won't exactly turn out the way your boss wants either.

The Flip Side: How to Get Yourself Fired—And Pay Attention, Overachievers

Getting fired is a jolting setback for anyone's career. Sometimes, the firing is a good wake-up call and becomes an opportunity to pursue something that would have otherwise not been pursued. Several very successful people in this book have been fired and bounced back.

Jamie Dimon, the CEO of JPMorgan, recalled the day he was fired by Sandy Weill. Up until his departure, he was one of Weill's loyal lieutenants, having helped his mentor build the behemoth of a company we now know as Citigroup.

"I was actually fine," Jamie reminisced. "It had been so unpleasant for so long and I tell people it was my net worth, not my self-worth, that was tied to the company. It was a little weird. All of the sudden I had gone from working ninety hours a week to zero . . . but I figured I was going to take the time and figure it out, and think it through, and hopefully learn from what happened. And I thought it was possible I might never get another job like that again. I wasn't naïve about that."

But most of us would rather not be on the receiving end of a firing. It can be very difficult to shake off the rejection. Future employers frown upon that history. Why burden yourself with this if you can help it?

Bruce Ratner summed up perfectly a primary reason why people are fired (save for issues like cheating, stealing, and harassment).

"The thing that is absolutely fatal is being lazy," Ratner said. "And I mean that in every kind of way. Lazy-minded, lazy with time and, I mean, it's a nasty word because there's iterations of it. You know who you are. You can try to hide it but before long everybody talks about it.

"There's a woman that works in our office who is not lazy-minded but she doesn't put in the greatest hours and I wish she'd learn she's not putting in a great day. But I can handle that. The other way around I can't handle. I cannot handle someone who's there twenty-four hours a day but doesn't really work, doesn't use up his lazy mind."

What was most stunning to hear is how many overachievers were fired or frowned upon because of another fatal flaw: They did not want to share.

"The irony or the paradox is the brighter somebody is, generally, the less willing they are to collaborate," Martin

Sorrell, the WPP advertising agency CEO, said. "Average people collaborate better than exceptional people. Then when all the average people want to be exceptional, they also become difficult and don't collaborate as well. So we get ourselves into a real pickle. But it is true that the better the person, the higher the probability that he or she will not share knowledge, share ability, share their experience with others."

In one case, that cost a person her job, as Sam Zell described.

"I hired this woman from a major corporation, and she was very, very smart. But I fired her within nine months. I promise you this woman had never been fired in her life; she was a major overachiever. But she brought an element from her past job in the corporate world that didn't fit with our culture. She used information as currency. The most important thing about an entrepreneurial world is that the enemy is without, not within. I can't have an employee who holds back information for political reasons or unless they are going to get something in return. We operate in a much too fast-paced environment for that kind of internal trading. In a big corporation, almost everything moves slowly so you have more time and opportunity to catch mistakes. That culture often breeds using information as currency. In an entrepreneurial culture, if somebody has information that they're not sharing with others in my shop, that means that I'm taking risks that I don't know about."

The reality is that most people who are fired already knew they were on the receiving line. There are very few cases when someone is fired that he or she did not already feel it in the gut. Make sure you stay tuned to that gut and know when to move on.

As Jamie put it: "When you love a company you want to do the right thing for that company. But I was becoming angry, which wouldn't be good for me or the company." That's when he knew he needed to move on.

And remember that this is not a situation that hits only junior employees. Sallie Krawcheck, the former head of Bank of America's private wealth management, who has been on both ends asking for and being demanded of raises, jokes: "When I used to do it, I used to break out in blotches so badly on my neck that my boss would feel sorry for me. As I tell folks, I finally invested in a turtleneck.

"But look, I always find [that being] fact-based, unemotional, helps in most situations. My management style was I embrace your opinion; I love to hear your opinion, make sure you give me your facts. The facts are stubborn things, and you can manage through facts, not through opinions."

So what do you do? How do you earn more?

The bigger question, I believe, is why do we feel so underpaid to begin with?

Well, consider that the gap between how much the person at the very top earns to the person at the very bottom is getting bigger and bigger. According to Bloomberg data, the average salary of a CEO, when taking into account all 500 companies in the Standard & Poor's index, was 204 times the salary of the average rank-and-file worker. That was up 20 percent since 2009. When digging into specific companies, Bloomberg found that the ousted former CEO of J.C. Penney, Ron Johnson, made 1,795 times more than the average department store employee. The next highest: Abercrombie & Fitch's CEO, who made 1,640 times more than the average clothing store retailer worker.

None of this is a judgment on pay—after all, that's up to the boards who put together the compensation packages for senior executives—but it is a partial explanation for why an air of inequality pervades almost every corporate office. When people ask for a raise it is precisely because they feel things are unfair. Harvey is absolutely right. But fair is very subjective. In every office, someone is always going to be making more than you who is similar in skill and dedication and someone is always going to be making less than you who may be putting more blood, sweat, and tears into his or her work. If money is "just a way of keeping score," as Texan oil tycoon H.L. Hunt once said, it's also a lousy, imperfect way to do so because compensation is such a lousy, imperfect system.

And so when you walk into that boss office asking for a raise, don't kid yourself that the primary motivation is financial—what you're really looking for is affirmation you're moving along in the game.

★★★★★★★★

In May 2013, the Pew Research Center put out the results of an amazing study. It found that mothers were the primary or only breadwinner in a record 40 percent of all U.S. households. That means almost half of all households in America have a woman as the main provider. I am myself in that category.

There was something to both feel good and bad about. On the one hand, women were boosting the standard of living for their children because in many cases, two incomes were rolling in. On the other, researchers found more women were living as single mothers and earning way below the national median family income. Women were simultaneously breaking inequality barriers and widening them.

In 1960, only 11 percent of households had women as the primary breadwinner. Think about that: In about a half-century, women breadwinners went from barely anything to 40 percent. In the next 20 years, a woman as the main provider won't be so remarkable anymore.

How does this relate to the "ask for a raise" question?

One consistent message I kept hearing from CEOs, managers, and executives was this: Women didn't know how to ask for a raise as well as a man. It wasn't sexist—it was nearly a fact. I say nearly because some men are pretty awful at it too. But in private, managers said to me that unfortunately, women did not speak up enough and were therefore, paid less.

Susan Lyne remembers how glaring this disparity was when she ran companies like Gilt Groupe, Martha Stewart Omnimedia, and ABC Entertainment: "Still to this day, I can count on one hand the number of women to come in and have the tough conversation with me, the 'I deserve more.' They wait until their review period and they may argue for that when their turn comes, but they will rarely step up out of line, out of order to say, 'Hey I need a raise' or 'I need a promotion,' and men do it all the time without thinking twice about it. I'm really saying this as an observation. I actually *like* the fact that people wait until the twice-a-year review period to say 'Okay, I've heard your comments about me, I really do feel like I nailed that job, I'm ready for responsibility and understand what career path there is for me.' I love that because I'm prepared for it at the moment. I will tell you that guys step out of that and they do end up getting promoted more. When you have to react to someone who says, 'I'm unhappy' and you don't want to lose that person, you proactively figure out a way to get them more responsibility."

Sallie Krawcheck had a similar experience, although not about raises. When she was the CEO of Smith Barney and ran the wealth management businesses at Bank of America and Citigroup, she controlled billions of dollars of clients' money. Her job was to find the right places to put that money. Billions of it.

"I was the belle of the ball and maybe not every week, but certainly every two weeks I would have somebody, a friend of mine, an acquaintance of mine, an acquaintance of an acquaintance, come to visit me, wanting to catch up," she recalled. "And I always knew what they were coming for. They'd always show up because they wanted a job or they [were a] hedge fund manager who wanted another platform, or a private equity manager who wanted a platform . . . and you go, like, okay, that's the game. That's fine. That's just part of the game.

"It struck me recently, those guys were coming in all the time. Do you know how many times it was a woman who came to my door to make that request?"

She made a "0" sign with her middle finger and thumb.

"*Zero*. In a decade? *Zero*. And so when you're looking at what is holding women back, some of it is that they weren't taking the risk of coming in and asking."

"Clearly female hedge fund managers were out there," I said.

"Absolutely. I'll take it even a step further. If they're going to come in, it should be to me, because I actually happen to be a woman."

When you consider that almost half the workers in the United States are now women, that's a lot of lost opportunity. As Tuck Business School professor Ella Edmondson Bell found in her research, women just fundamentally differ in how they approach work than men. In some of her findings, which she described at a Harvard University symposium in March of 2013, she said "too many women believe performance is the only criteria for advancing in their organizations so they don't build critical relationships." She also said that of the more

than 60 women she observed who graduated from a leadership program, many were "really smart" but "lacked confidence in themselves"
and didn't have "much patience to 'hang in' until they are promoted."

"Too many of the women lack critical assignments that will give
them 'star' visibility in their companies, even though they are considered high potential," she said. "Such assignments enable a woman to
prove herself by showcasing her skills, tenacity, leadership, and making a
difference to the company's bottom line."

Contrast that with what Fred Kofman said, that the only way to
earn a higher salary is "for you to be more valuable to your employer
than anyone else who could do your job" and it's a wonder to see why
some women just don't have the confidence to barge into a boss' office
and demand a raise.

★★★★★★★★

Remember I mentioned that I'd taken the first salary offer once and
it was a big mistake (as my boss mentioned to me much later, after the
contract was signed and sealed). Let me tell you what happened.

I'd just finished my maternity leave and I was still hell bent on
switching careers from newspapers to television. Finally, it seemed I
was near an offer. Despite my gut telling me to stay unemotional, I was
so overcome by fear that if I didn't take this job, my career was over. I
remember sitting up all night waiting for the offer letter to arrive.

When it finally did, I immediately frowned at the salary proposal.
It was much lower than what I'd expected and doing a quick calcula-
tion in my head, I'd barely be saving any money. In fact, I was probably
going to end up "paying" for the privilege of the job. I had two children to feed and was barely saving any money at the end of the month.
But I was so frightful this was the best I could get that I accepted the
offer without hesitation.

Years later, as I was transitioning to the next job, my boss—a
woman—sat down with me for a good-bye drink and said, "You know
Betty, one thing that I've always wanted to say to you is . . . you should
never have taken that first offer. You really surprised me when you did.
You could have easily gotten more."

What she said did not surprise me. I already knew I had sold myself
short. I knew I was making less than my co-workers. For two years, I

reasoned that the amount of money I'd missed out on was the collateral damage I needed to absorb in exchange for the security of the job.

It was a valuable lesson to have learned. And at the time, it was a lesson I could afford to learn—not because I could literally afford to live on the salary but because I was still way ahead of my peak earning years. Whatever salary mistakes I made I could offset them later. I might not have thought that way if I was, say, 50 years old.

Most of us will follow a similar earnings trajectory. It's amazing when I looked at the charts how typical and patterned our lives really are—how herd-like and organized we are in the way we all follow similar paths. Perhaps much to Glenn Hutchins' satisfaction, very few of us *putz* around in our 20s and 30s and try to climb out of a hole. Most of us climb the mountain to the peak—the time when we earn the most, which is in our 40s and 50s.

Glenn's mountain metaphor made me think of a bicycle trail I've ridden almost every weekend. It's just near my house in an area known as the South Mountain Reservation. On Sundays, the police block off the road so that cyclists and runners can exercise without worrying about traffic. At first, I could hardly get up the hills—there was one particularly long and grueling one—but after a few weeks, I started to cycle up the road with less effort. My favorite part was flying down, which instantly made me feel like I was 10 years old. Once I got past my own exercise inertia, I began to notice the other people on the road. They were mostly regulars like me. There were the spindly, bare-legged guys decked out in their cycling gear flying past me. Then the parents with the toddlers in strollers. One guy in a green shirt and black shorts would walk up and down the road kicking a soccer ball all the way, eyes never off the ball. There could be naked women around him and he would be oblivious. Fat people, skinny people, old men and young ladies all on bicycles or jogging, challenging themselves and charting their own paths but following a general course. I started to call it The Road of Life after what Glenn told me. Sometimes my boys would join me on their bicycles and then the metaphor really hit. We were all trying to make it up the mountain—some harder than others—until we reached the point where we had to turn around. But once you made it up to the peak you knew going down would be easy and fun.

According to the Georgetown University Center on Education and the Workforce, no matter what degree or education you have, between the ages of 40 and 44 is when a person's income is the highest. Of course the level of education matters in showing how much *more* you're earning. If you're a high school dropout, you're earning just 19 percent more in your 40s than when you first started out. If you have a professional degree, you're earning 100 percent more than you did when you first began.

That tells me two things. One is that education counts. And two is that in your 20s and early 30s is when you can take some risks because you're not risking very much; but that when you're in your 50s and 60s and you take a risk, you will have a very difficult time catching up to your peers.

When I read through this, I got a little depressed. As a woman, I already had to deal with a biological clock, the last thing I wanted to think about was a salary-earning clock. I'd like to believe in my idealistic way that no matter how old you are, the potential for great success and earnings is there. The American Dream has no expiration date.

And it does—to a degree. When I started to think back, I realized I made my biggest leaps and bounds in salary when I was younger, not because I made so much money but because a doubling of salary is pretty easy to achieve if you're making $25,000 a year. When you're at the bottom of the mountain, you want to get to that peak fast. The result is that later on, when you're making a more substantial salary, a 10 percent raise is going to mean so much more in dollar terms than a 10 percent raise on $25,000.

So when I think about other people and their hesitations with asking for a raise, it must be remembered that if you don't snag an opportunity while you can *risk the most*, you'll end up way behind on the pay scale. Forget about making sure you are paid more than your peers in the office—what's most important is that you're accelerating your pay and working towards a bigger and bigger salary. I knew I was doing that when I actually stepped *back* in my pay and took the television job. I knew it would contribute to my overall value later. Rather than ask the same old question, "How do I ask for a raise?" the bigger and more strategic question is, "How do I earn the most out of my career?"

And then you start doing it.

I mentioned before that there really are basic pointers to consider when asking for a raise. But below are four things that may help you prepare yourself better when you walk into the boss' office.

1. It's Not Personal, It's Just Business.

The Godfather was right: Being as unemotional as you can be will benefit you more than you realize. It'll make you sound more cogent and organized. Sometimes it helps to go in thinking you're advocating for someone else (the next chapter explains this more fully). But don't be hard on yourself if you do get emotional about this—the idea is you want to try to stay as fact-based as possible and take out all the insecurities and fears.

2. You Make Money, I Make Money.

I mentioned before the idea that getting a raise depended on how valuable you were to the company. But think about how valuable you are overall to the people around you. The more valuable you make yourself, the more likely your earnings will rise. And I'm not just talking about at the office but to your network of colleagues and acquaintances. The more valuable you make yourself to them, the more likely you'll rise in value yourself. It's a halo effect of value.

David Kerpen, the CEO of Likeable Media, mentioned to me how he'd helped a father at his daughter's school with advice on publishing a book. "I gave him some of my time and I said this is exactly how I can help you promote the book. He said 'What do I owe you for this? What do I pay you?' and I said don't worry about it," Kerpen said. A little while later, a company hired Kerpen's firm and it wasn't until later he'd learned it was on the recommendation of this same father. Examples like that are everywhere.

3. Know When to Hit the Road.

I hate the word *quit*. Quitting your job is like quitting the game. Look at it more as know when you need to move on to a better place. Sometimes people outgrow their jobs. Sometimes they're passed over for promotions. Corporate executive suites are flush with dramas of people who've been pushed aside or passed over for top jobs and who then move onto something else. When Jack Welch picked Jeff Immelt to succeed him at General Electric, Jim McNerney and Robert Nardelli went on to take CEO jobs elsewhere (the former went to 3M and then Boeing and the latter went to Home Depot).

Jamie Dimon was famously fired from Citigroup after he clashed with the legendary Wall Street CEO Sandy Weill, reportedly for being too ambitious. A few years later, JPMorgan under Jamie Dimon soared above the other banks in the financial crisis while Citigroup disintegrated under its bad debts.

At 30, Steve Jobs was also publicly fired from Apple. In his must-watch Stanford University commencement address, he called it one of the best things that ever happened to him.

"The heaviness of being successful was replaced by the lightness of being a beginner again, less sure about everything. It freed me to enter one of the most creative periods of my life," he told the graduating students. "I'm pretty sure none of this would have happened if I hadn't been fired from Apple. It was awful-tasting medicine, but I guess the patient needed it."

The thing to remember is not to burn any bridges when you do quit or leave the firm. Even if you absolutely hated the place where you were or felt miserable there, you always want to leave a positive impression.

Nolan Bushnell: Steve Jobs' First Boss on Paying Well

Nolan Bushnell has the distinction of being Steve Jobs first and only boss when he hired him in 1974 at Atari. Nolan went on to start several businesses, not all related to technology. He has probably made millions of children—and parents—everywhere happy on a rainy Sunday with his Chuck E. Cheese pizza–video game arcade concept (the company later went into bankruptcy after he left to start other ventures).

Nolan had just written a book, *Finding the Next Steve Jobs: How to Find, Hire, Keep and Nurture Creative Talent*, that looked at corporate culture. As would be expected from someone who's always colored outside the lines, Nolan is not impressed with the way companies motivate workers. On compensation he writes: "If you want to feel like you want to drain the last nickel out of somebody, that's where you lose loyalty. If the minute somebody offers one of my employees a salary that's higher than what I'm paying them, then that's my mistake. I haven't properly evaluated the market.

"I try to get people to view their compensation as part of stock plans. It's very interesting, anybody who's ever made money values stock options highly. If they never before made money, then they don't value them very much. What I've done is to constantly have that money off the table. I don't want people thinking whether they're being well paid or not. I want it to be a given that they're making more money than their friends and I tell [my employees] all the time, I say if anybody feels like they can get better money somewhere else, let me know, give me the chance to match it."

4. Write Yourself a Check.

People are often focused on their next raise. Why not focus on your overall earnings potential? What can you do now to lay the groundwork for a bigger salary later? According to that Georgetown University study, a person with a high school diploma can expect to earn about $1.3 million over a lifetime. Someone with a bachelor's degree can earn about $2.3 million over a lifetime. How do you exceed that goal? What can be done to reach bigger lifetime earnings?

One story that I read always stuck in my mind. Jack Canfield is the author of those syrupy *Chicken Soup for the Soul* books that's netted him a gazillion dollars and made him a Guinness Book World Record holder for having seven books simultaneously on the *New York Times* bestseller list. His books may be touchy-feely but his success story is hardcore serious. Canfield has recounted in interviews how many times his book idea was rejected before finally someone took a gamble on it. In less than a year, he'd been given his first $1 million check from the publisher. One thing Canfield also recounts is his decision to write himself those million dollar checks before they actually appeared. He did so when in one year, on a lark, he decided to write himself a check for $100,000. And before he knew it, by the end of that year, he'd actually almost earned $100,000 despite having a salary of just $8,000. His next goal? $1 million.

Voodoo magic? Not really. The concept is not terribly different from a company CEO who says in 12 months he plans to see the company earning X amount of money. It's visualizing what the goal is and then setting in motion the things to make it happen. It can work for companies who are laser-focused and it can also work for you. Sometimes just writing down the numbers on a piece of paper and looking at it every day is enough to get you focused.

Chapter 5

The Art of Negotiation

For the most part, we're negotiating throughout our whole lives. At work, we're negotiating for better jobs and assignments; outside of work, we're negotiating for our next car or house; as a parent, we're constantly negotiating with our kids and babysitters. If you don't know the basics of negotiation, you'll lose out.

I don't negotiate billion-dollar deals, but Sam Zell, a billionaire, does. So I asked him how he approaches negotiating.

"There's only one way to negotiate a good deal and that is to understand what it is that the other guy needs," Sam said. "If you can prioritize his needs then you can respond to him in a manner that's likely to create a high probability of success. Obviously the other part of that equation is you have to know what's on the table that you absolutely have to have. So if I've done my homework, and I realize that I can't give the guy across the table what he has to have, I'll end the negotiations quickly. There's no point to continue. This is not a torture test.

"I had a banker at the Continental Bank who had an orange sign on the corner of his desk, and the orange sign said, 'Fastest NO in the

West.' And I loved it. We've tried really hard to run our business on that premise. Fastest NO in the West," he continued. "I once made a deal with Carl Icahn to buy his railcar business. I walked out of Carl's office and said to the guy who came with me, 'He's going to call tomorrow and renege,' and he did. I knew it was a deal Carl wasn't going to be able to live with. It was the damnest thing. In this particular situation, I understood immediately that the deal he was saying he was going to do, he just couldn't do it, and he didn't."

Jimmy Lee, the consummate Wall Street dealmaker, agrees. "Sometimes the best advice is to recommend walking away and not do the deal," he said. "Other times, you need to push your very hardest to see two sides come together. That's what I did with Brian Roberts and Jeff Immelt on the sale of NBC [from General Electric to Comcast]. I knew it was the right deal for both sides and it was."

In his latest book, *It Worked for Me*, General Colin Powell, a man who has negotiated with heads of state, commanded the first Gulf War, and faced down the Russians, said he learned something about negotiating from a bunch of lawyers. He writes:

Back in 1978, working as a staff assistant to Secretary of Defense Harold Brown during the Carter administration, I had to referee a heated dispute over some obscure issue. I sat at the head of the table in Secretary Brown's conference room filled with people and listened to two lawyers go at each other. They quickly got past the merits and demerits of the issue, but the debate continued, and for one of the lawyers it became increasingly personal. As he grew more and more agitated, he got himself tied up in arguments about how the outcome would affect him. I finally lost patience and stopped the debate. I'd heard enough. I decided the issue in favor of the other lawyer, based on the strength of his presentation and reasoning.

The fellow who lost looked crushed, to the discomfort of everyone in the room. The other lawyer looked at him and said, "Never let your ego get so close to your position that when your position falls, your ego goes with it." In short, accept that your position was faulty, not your ego.

I love this topic because I think for many people, especially women, negotiating is seen as an alpha male, in-your-face ritual of corporate life aggrandized in Hollywood movies and bestsellers like *Barbarians at the Gate*. For some people, especially those on Wall Street, it is exactly like that. For others like you and me, it's simply trying to figure out what we both want and how to get it. Understanding how negotiating works can do wonders for your career.

There are three basics I've learned from some of the best negotiators on what produces the best outcome:

1. Know what the other party wants.
2. Listen very carefully.
3. Don't let your emotions get in the way of a deal.

These are also, by the way, the basics for being a very good salesman.

Of those three, Jim Reynolds, the CEO of the boutique investment bank and former star bond salesman for Merrill Lynch, said listening is extremely important, if not *the* most important skill of any good negotiator.

"I would say that ninety percent of people do not ever perfect the art of listening nor do they ever learn how important listening is to virtually anything, but especially business," he said. "My first job was with IBM in the early 1980s. IBM trained you for nine months before you actually did anything. That training primarily consisted of learning technology, but if you were slated to go into sales, which I was, you learned how to sell. They taught you two secrets on how to sell. Those two were how to ask questions and how to listen, because if you can ask questions and you can listen, as a salesman, you will know everything you need to know about how to sell your product. I'll give you some examples because there was a lot of role-playing in this training. You could tap anyone on the shoulder and do a trial sales call with them. They pretend they're the client and have every objection to buying a computer. You had to be serious and pitch to them. What you learned to ask are things like, 'Okay, Mr. Customer, if you automate this process, and instead of twelve people doing it, you had two people, what would you do with that additional staff?' Or 'Mr. Customer, if you could do this in one hour instead of twelve, how would that increase productivity in your business?' You ask open-ended questions—never ask a yes or no question—and listen to the answer. What would happen is if I asked those questions, I would get explanations on what the issues were for the client and if you sopped up everything, all you did was say back to them what they just told you was important to them."

I had to admit the image that came to mind when Jim started describing the IBM sales trainees was the typical cocky, off-putting sales guy you see in television shows and on used car sales lots: guys in plaid shirt sleeves sitting around *The Office*.

"No, the secret to effective selling is not the guy who goes in talking 'I can do I this and I can do that and I can make your business better.' That was never the guy who was the top salesman. The top salesman was always the guy that could ask leading questions and then listen to the answer. I learned this early on in my twenties and I'm still trying to teach it to my bankers. I have fifteen-, twenty-year veterans on my staff and the biggest thing I have to teach them is know when to keep quiet. You should start actually paying attention to people, in a group, see how much *real* listening is going on. Whoever is doing the real listening is improving the art of effective communication and that person will get even better."

It's no surprise Jim is not only sealing deals left and right across the country but that he's also a very popular business figure in Chicago, well known as someone who helped President Barack Obama get his start in politics. He is, by the way, a pure entrepreneur, always on the move—every time we talk he's at a party, sports game, plane, or a conference meeting new people and connecting the dots.

Elon Musk: I Like to Listen to Negative Feedback

Elon, as you can tell, is already an unusual CEO and a well-admired entrepreneur. When we got on the subject of listening, Elon said he always listens to his critics, even if they are doing things like holding a "deathwatch" over his company.
Elon said he makes it a point to listen to the negative.

Elon: I think it's important for people to pay close attention to negative feedback and rather than ignore negative feedback, you have to listen to it carefully. Ignore it if the underlying reason for the negative feedback doesn't make sense but otherwise, people should adjust their behavior. I'm not perfect at it, for sure, but I do think it's really important to solicit negative feedback, particularly from people who have your best interest in mind.

Me: But that's just putting yourself open to criticism. People may think that makes them look vulnerable or weak.

Elon: I think that I would recommend the opposite. I think that you should always be seeking negative feedback. Positive feedback you'll get automatically, particularly if it's a friend. They're happy to praise or compliment you on something, but they are less likely to tell you if you're doing something stupid. They don't want you to feel bad.

Me: How do you solicit the negative feedback?

Elon: I ask specifically what am I doing wrong. And if I've asked that a few times of people, then they will start automatically telling me without me having to always ask the question. So like for the Model S, I said I don't really want to know what's right about the car. I want to know what's wrong with the car.

Me: Nobody wants to hear that.

Elon: Exactly. But one has to take one's medicine.

In another part of the country, Lew Dickey, based in Atlanta and the head of the radio station owner Cumulus, whose star talent includes Rush Limbaugh, agrees that listening is the key to any good deal.

"People make the mistake of somebody's talking and all they're doing is waiting for them to finish so they can say what they want to say," he said. "Sometimes people are too concerned about getting their point out. They're not listening at what's coming back. It's the advice I give our people: Don't be in such a hurry to get your point out, listen to what the other person tells you because oftentimes they'll guide you. If you listen, they'll guide you on how to sell to them. They'll guide you on how to negotiate with them, if you listen carefully."

He also prepares as much as possible, doing his own research so that he goes into any deal knowing what the other side really wants.

Richard Branson, the dashing founder of the Virgin Group, wrote in a blog posting in September 2012 about the "Rules for Being a Good Negotiator." Richard wrote:

> Roger Fisher, a great conflict negotiator and peacemaker, died last month aged 90. His rules for being a good negotiator were pointed out in *The Economist*: "In any negotiation, he wrote—even with the terrorists—it was vital to separate the people from the problem; to focus on the underlying interests of both sides, rather than stake out unwavering positions; and to explore all possible options before making a decision. The parties should try to build a rapport, check each other out, even just by shaking hands or eating together. Each should 'listen actively,' as he always did, to what the other was saying. They should recognize the emotions on either side, from a longing for security to a craving for status. And they should try to get inside each other's heads."

In those two paragraphs, Richard Branson summed up the three rules of a good negotiation that I listed earlier:

1. Know what the other party wants.
2. Listen carefully.
3. Don't let your emotions get in the way of a good deal.

That's largely what the first rule of negotiation is about—understanding what the other party wants and giving it to them without costing yourself more than you can afford. In his famous tome, *The 7 Habits of Highly Effective People*, Stephen Covey wrote about the winner-takes-all attitude that is as pervasive in corporate culture 20-plus years ago as it is today. In it, he wrote the best negotiations happen when, rather than win/lose, both parties strike a win/win. He wrote:

Because Win/Win is a principle people can validate in their own lives, you will be able to bring most people to a realization that they win more of what they want by going for what you both want. But there will be a few who are so deeply embedded in the Win/Lose mentality that they just won't think Win/Win. So remember that No Deal is always an option.

And that made me think of Sam Zell again: Fastest NO in the West.

****

Listening is my job. Without trying to be boastful, I have always been a good listener, which is what I think has helped me be a good reporter. When I was a newspaper reporter, it often happened that I would interview the same people other reporters did and stay twice as long, with the interviewee often proclaiming what a good listener I was.

A majority of the time most of what people were telling me was not usable but I was always waiting for something said which would spark an idea or a connection. Or in other instances, I was volunteering myself to be the sounding board for people who wanted to get a story or opinion off their chest. And you know who was the happiest knowing this? Not me, but the person who just spent an hour talking because somebody was there to listen. Listening is always a way to connect with someone.

Listening is critical in my job. When guests come onto my program and we have five minutes to cover one topic, I have to really listen to what the guest is saying because oftentimes, the most interesting answers don't come in your initial questions, but in your follow-ups.

People have asked me before what it's like to try to focus on listening to the guest while having producers talk in your ear. Here's a sampling of what it's like during a live broadcast:

Me: We'd like to welcome X to the program, thanks for joining us.
Guest: Thank you.
Me: Let's start with why you say the President should give companies a tax break so they can bring all their money back to the U.S.
Guest: Well, the President knows full well . . .
Producer in ear: Four minutes [to commercial break].

Me: But we've tried it before and it didn't work . . .

Guest: That's not true, it actually did create jobs, if you look back at the . . .

Producer in ear: Check your e-mail.

Me: [Reading e-mail and listening.]

Producer in ear: You want to do that? Shake your head yes or no.

Guest: And you know what, I know of two companies who say they'll create two thousand jobs total if they get the tax break.

Me: [In my head: What?] Two companies? Who?

Producer: A minute to break.

Guest: I can't say, but they're companies you'd know right off the bat . . .

Producer: Thirty seconds to break.

Guest continues to talk.

(Director jumps in: Got to cut him off! Fifteen seconds to break!)

Me: Well, X, thank you so much for joining us. Stay with us for more on [insert topic here].

Director: Three, two, one . . .

Has being a good listener helped me be a better negotiator? Not if I don't keep the other factors in mind, including knowing what the other side wants. And that comes by doing your homework.

Some of this relates to the prior chapter when we talked about asking for a raise. When you walk into your boss' office you should already be armed with a good amount of knowledge of what your boss' bottom line is going to be in giving you a raise. You should be knowledgeable about what's going on in your department and the company and how that might affect his or her reply. Having that knowledge is critical for any good negotiation.

One of the best examples that drove home the importance of listening happened at a football game. Not just any football game, but the Super Bowl. Jim, who as I mentioned was a mover and shaker, always finds himself in the heart of the action and, one February, he invited me down to New Orleans to catch the game. It was—as you could well imagine—a big party down in the French Quarter and the last place I thought I'd ever find myself. It was also the last place I thought I'd learn a business lesson.

On my first night, I went with Jim and his whole entourage of CEOs and ex-CEOs and ex-football players to a back room in an upscale, French Quarter restaurant. Sitting in the middle of some round tables was—who else?—the rapper/musician Jay Z, looking calm and welcoming. Timbaland, his fellow musician, was also there. There must have been twenty of us. I was too starry-eyed to really feel self-conscious. The conversation quickly became loud and raucous—the ex-football Hall of Famers judging whether quarterback Colin Kaepernick could really do it for the San Francisco 49ers the next day, why defense was more important than offense (no surprise given we were dining with linebackers), and as we drank Jay Z's D'Usse cognac and ate Oysters Rockefeller, I observed that out of all the guys in that room, Jay Z—the host and star—was one of the quietest. He was very attentive, turning his head to whoever was talking and responding when asked and laughing along but he must have been the fourth or fifth quietest guy in the room.

Later, Jim and I talked about that night and he agreed that Jay Z bore all the marks of a good listener.

"I was with him the night before you came and he was the same way. He just sat there and soaked it all in," Jim said. "He listens. It made me think of all the things he's done and the range of all that he has. Many of the things he's done, buying companies and building brands and representing athletes, so much of that goes to the power of listening."

Months later, the Jay Z brand only got bigger. He started a sports agency, Roc Nation Sports, and signed New York Yankees second baseman Robinson Cano as his first big client. Along with the numerous products he created, including the fashion line Rocawear, he partnered with the South Korean technology company Samsung to sell his latest album, *Magna Carta*, which made it an instant bestseller upon release.

In an interview with Anthony DeCurtis for *Men's Health*, Jay Z said: "I'm hungry for knowledge. The whole thing is to learn every day, to get brighter and brighter. That's what this world is about. You look at someone like Gandhi, and he glowed. Martin Luther King glowed. Muhammad Ali glows. I think that's from being bright all the time, and trying to be brighter. . . . That's what you should be doing your whole time on the planet. Then you feel like, 'My life is worth everything. And yours is too.'"

★★★★★★★★

Are men better negotiators than women?

I had to ask that question as I was researching this chapter. Most of the advice on negotiation came from men, men who were clearly alpha-male dealmakers and sales guys. I asked Lew Dickey if he'd ever negotiated with a woman and, with fork in hand, mid-bite, Lew looked a little surprised across the lunch table when he realized, "You know what? I can't recall ever having negotiated with a woman."

A Harvard Business School study done in 2006 provided a few answers. The researchers told the story of a woman named Maureen Park, the managing director of a small portfolio management firm. The woman was faced with low morale among her staff and two of her best analysts—both women—were becoming increasingly frustrated that their pay was substantially lower than their male counterparts. The women were doing just as hard a job but were being paid far less.

Maureen went to her bosses at the firm and fought to get the two women raises and to her surprise, the researchers noted, she got the increase in pay for them.

The researchers wrote:

> Reflecting on her triumph, Park realized with bitter irony that three of her seven direct reports would make more than she would in the coming year; she herself had accepted a small cost-of-living raise without question. If getting a raise was so easy, why hadn't she made a case for herself? Is it possible that her gender somehow influenced how Park negotiated for herself and others?

What the researchers found was . . . sort of—but not in the way that you would think.

It turns out men and women are equally good at negotiating when there is a concrete framework. A group of MBA students who know what the starting salaries and pay scales are in certain companies will pretty much all negotiate nearly the same starting salaries. But the Harvard researchers found that when MBA students were negotiating salaries where the starting pay was more ambiguous, men were able to get about $10,000 more than the women. "It's not that the pressure of competition causes women to stumble but, rather, that men step up their performance in competitive situations," they wrote.

In other words, when the situation turns into an "every man for himself" game—get whatever you can grab—the men snatch the ball and run with it.

Does that mean men are better negotiators? Not exactly, as the example of Maureen Park illustrates.

Along with Linda Babcock from Carnegie Mellon University, the Harvard researchers asked a group of executives to negotiate pay—one half were to negotiate the salary for someone else and the other half for themselves.

It turns out the women scored a salary that was 18 percent higher when they negotiated the salary for someone else. Men pretty much negotiated the same salaries whether it was for themselves or for someone else, and the levels were pretty consistent with what the women negotiated when they represented someone else.

"It appears that the women executives were particularly energized when they felt a sense of responsibility to represent another person's interests," the researchers concluded. "Just as men excel in ambiguous, competitive environments, women are exemplary negotiators when the beneficiary is someone other than themselves."

Incredibly, just as I was researching this, a Bloomberg data report came out that showed that women in the C-suite—the very top layer of management—suffered from an average 18 percent pay gap compared to men. There was something about the number 18. And there was definitely something going on that worked against women when they were negotiating raises for themselves. When I asked Carol Hymowitz, the author of the report, why this was, she said it's because women fail to negotiate the higher pay at an early age. That gap stays with them even when they become senior executives and even CEOs.

"I will say that women in general have a tougher time presenting themselves and being vocal in showcasing what they do than men," says Sheila Marcelo, the CEO of Care.com. "One of the things I try to encourage through role modeling is give women positive affirmations when they advocate for themselves. I may or may not necessarily give it to them but I will say, 'I want to tell you I love that you advocated' and constantly reaffirm that so they continue."

"And what about you," I asked. "Do you sometimes feel it's harder being a woman CEO?"

"I don't normally feel it. I felt it from vendors because I look young. Vendors will come in and not realize I am the decision maker and this was even before I was a CEO, because I look the youngest," she continued.

"They come in and say, 'Where's the boss?'" I asked.

"Yes and they don't realize it. Then when you're at parity around the conversation, they start to realize I think she's the decision maker and it surprises them. That's typically what I've just done in the past is just focus on the conversation and just get to it."

All of this made me think back again to the Roger Fisher quote— "it was vital to separate the people from the problem"—and how it appears *that* is the primary problem for women. It's difficult for us to separate the person from the problem, the person being ourselves. It is likely why so many of us are short changed in our pay and in our desires for what we'd like.

So for women, perhaps the quote above is actually the most critical. How do we keep our own emotions in check and not let them get in the way of a good deal?

Part Two

The Three Fs:
Fear, Finances, and Flow

Chapter 6

Fear

People who know me well know I hate to fly.

Apparently, according to a survey by Boeing dating back to 1980 (surveys on fear of flying are very sparse), about a third of Americans hate to fly, too.

I have no real justification. I have never been in a near-death experience on a plane (knock on wood). The worst experience was one I missed. In 1983, my family was scheduled to be on the same Korean Airlines plane that got shot down by Soviet missiles.

The Boeing 747 had been on its way from New York to Seoul when it strayed into forbidden Soviet airspace. Luckily, my parents had changed their minds about the trip a few weeks before.

Every time a plane takes off, I stare at the flight attendants. If they look calm, I feel calm. And usually they are. One time I was in a tiny commuter plane from New York to Philadelphia—the kind with one row of seats on one side and two on the other. The space was so tight that when the flight attendant was sitting in his jump seat, he was practically on our laps. Before takeoff, he closed the door by propping his right foot on the side wall and pulling the door in repeatedly until it squeezed shut—like what you do when you're pulling an overstuffed suitcase through a too-small hole. Then the flight attendant smoothed over the duct tape that was all over the door, apparently meant to plug up any cracks. The condition of the door made me turn to the passenger next to me, a young Indian man, whose eyes grew big and mouth let out a little "Oh!" But throughout the trip, the flight attendant looked calm and confident, as if a duct-taped airplane door that wouldn't shut properly was absolutely normal for all of us. And it was, at least on that night. The flight landed on time and in one piece.

My fear of flying made me dig a little deeper into fear. Fear, as we may all suspect, is a chemical reaction in our brain that's located in the hypothalamus. For some reason, our brains make us all react to frightening situations with the same "face of fear." You know that face when you see a spider—your eyes widen and your mouth automatically gaps open. Charles Darwin and other evolutionary scientists tried to figure out why we all expressed fear this way. Some conjectured the opening of the eyes made us see better and that the opening of the mouth led us to breathe deeper so we could energize our bodies. Others said it was a look to serve as a warning for others: If you see fear all over someone's face, you're going to get the hell out of there too.

Statistics on people's fears are hard to come by. A widely quoted study is contained in the 1977 edition of *The Book of Lists*, which reported a person's number one fear is public speaking. Death came in at number seven. This led to one of Jerry Seinfeld's famous, if slightly inaccurate, jokes: "According to most studies, people's number one fear is public speaking. Number two is death. Death is number two. Does that sound right? This means to the average person, if you go to a funeral, you're better off in the casket than doing the eulogy," he joked.

A 2001 Gallup poll listed snakes as the number one fear and flying as number eight, with death not making the list at all. And yet another widely quoted poll—the National Comorbidity Survey—says animals or bugs are a number one fear while flying is number nine.

If you talk to therapists and anyone else who has dealt with people's fears, the best way to overcome that fear is to face it. Some people who are afraid of snakes are asked to eventually hold, maybe even kiss, a snake. Some who are afraid to speak publicly are asked to do it while imagining the audience naked. For my part, I have come up with my own solution to facing the fear of flying because there's no avoiding it. I usually buy a load of trashy magazines so I can entertain myself throughout the flight; I watch the flight attendants hoping that face of fear never blooms; and I count how many rows to the exit door. It's my way of taking control of a situation that I basically have no control over.

Why all this talk about fear?

I found when talking with CEOs that fear was a pervasive emotion in all their careers. Some said it held people back in their careers. Others said it motivated them, like Sam Zell. One person you wouldn't expect to have a lot of fear is the young brash billionaire, Elon Musk, who's built two companies at the same time—Tesla, the electric car maker, and SpaceX, the private space rocket company.

"I feel fear really strongly," he told me one Saturday from his SpaceX headquarters just outside Los Angeles. "It's quite unpleasant."

"What were you fearful about?" I asked him.

"For several years the companies were on the brink of extinction and I sort of felt quite a lot of fear for the companies not living. And 2007, '08, and '09 were just terrible, terrible years. The companies were just clinging on to existence by their fingernails, basically. I had so many sleepless nights and a great deal of fear."

What was left unsaid by Elon was that shortly after that, in 2010, the press began reporting that not only were his companies running into trouble, but *he* was hitting financial bottom from a contentious public divorce. The *New York Times* reported he was broke after a court filing and quoted Elon as writing: "About four months ago, I ran out of cash." He was sleeping on friends' couches and borrowing money. It was juicy gossip for the tech and business press.

Getting back to the conversation, I said: "That's an understandable fear but most people have a fear that prevents them from doing things. A fear of failure," I said.

"Yes, I don't have a fear of failure," he continued. "I'm not going to fail to do something just because I fear that I wouldn't win. Particularly if it's something that I think is really important to the future. When I started SpaceX and Tesla . . . I would have given the odds of success at less than 50 percent. Significantly less, probably. But even though the probability of success was low, it was still worth doing. Right now I have relatively low fear because I think [the companies] are in pretty good shape. So if I were to have fear about the companies, I think it would be disproportionate to the reality.

"I think people often are just irrational about fears. Before SpaceX and Tesla, even though I thought the most likely outcome was failure, that didn't mean that I would be destitute. Even when I invested the last money that I had to keep Tesla alive and had to borrow money from friends just to pay rent . . . there were all sorts of blogs keeping a Tesla deathwatch. It was terrible. It was just constantly beating the heck out of me. It was quite awful."

"So what got you through that?" I asked.

"I thought I had an obligation to do everything possible to make Tesla and SpaceX succeed because I think they're important to the future of the world. And I don't want to have to look back on that and say, 'Well, you know, there's one thing I could have done and I didn't do it and maybe if we had done that we would have succeeded.' I didn't want that to be the case."

"So it was more like you feared the regret rather than the failure," I said.

"Yes, exactly."

Put another way, Elon Musk has a high tolerance for risk, which means his fear is not of failing but of not taking the risk for the biggest reward. That's a fear many entrepreneurs have and it's why so many of them—Richard Branson, Mark Zuckerberg, Bill Gates, Steve Jobs—build the companies that they do.

John Chambers, the CEO of Cisco, a huge technology company that employs over 65,000 people, was very frank about how risk-taking can be a positive thing to encourage, but that it also comes with many consequences.

"I think any business leader who doesn't take risk will not be successful, so everybody's going to have areas they like to have a do-over or something that didn't play out the way they wanted," he said. "For me, it's almost always around not moving fast enough. Every move that got me into trouble is when I haven't moved fast enough, not because I moved too fast."

"Why did that happen?" I asked.

"Sometimes it was allowing my team to collaborate on an issue too long and not pushing them to a decision. Other times it can be, well, that's risky and where does it fit into my priorities, because you can only take so many priorities at one time depending on how fast you're growing or not. And in today's times especially, you can only take so many of those risks because, Betty, if you take even something that is as high as seventy percent odds and you do three of them, your chances on being successful with all three of them . . . are one chance in three. And if you're in a market that's growing slow and that third one is very visible, it didn't work, that can cost the CEO their job."

Sam Zell on Fear and Money:

"Fear is an incredibly important part of [my entrepreneurial career]. There's a correlation between fear and using your own money. In other words, if I'm using your money or your pension and I'm investing it, I may have less fear than if it's my own money. When I wrote a check for $300 million to the *Chicago Tribune*, that was my money. And it's gone!"—Sam Zell.

The reality is that most of us, unless we live in a cave in the middle of nowhere, will fail at something. My earliest memory of failing began in childhood when I was in the fourth grade. I qualified for a *Jeopardy* game show staged in front of the entire school. My parents were sitting right in the middle of the auditorium in the front row, watching intently. I was the youngest person to be chosen to compete and I knew how proud my parents were. As the game got going, I quickly buzzed in my first answer, which was wrong. I buzzed a few more times and got the answers wrong again and again. In fact, all my answers were wrong with a capital *W*. It got to the point I could feel my teammates glaring at me to stop buzzing and losing them points. My parents' faces went from genuine proud smiles to frozen "we-better-keep-the-same-expressions-or-else-she'll-know" smiles. At the end, my parents found me and gave me a sympathetic pat on the back, with a "you did good" comment that I knew was, for all their efforts to shield me from hurt feelings, simply not true. I guess you could say once I got on stage, I choked.

But that's grade school. Let's talk about failing with real consequences, like the kind where you lose your job or your savings. That fear is very real because almost all of us have encountered or been the subject of a failure like that. Some people have such a fear of this that it's been given a medical name: atychiphobia. That's an extreme form of fear that prevents people from doing anything that would risk failure. Imagine what a terribly limiting life you'd have. The only safe thing you'd be doing was sitting on the couch watching *Jeopardy*.

Most of us have some form of this condition, a running dialogue that constantly helps us evaluate whether we commit to something or not. It's actually not a bad thing. Imagine if you had absolutely no fear and you just took risks all the time, you'd probably end up bankrupt or dead. I think about those people who have the unusual condition of feeling no pain—they have absolutely no fear about putting their hands on a stove or climbing up a tree and then breaking their leg falling down. Fear gives us some perspective.

Ultimately, fear is a unique paradox. It is what both motivates and limits you, it forces you to both stretch and contain your boundaries, it is energizing and depleting. It's such a complicated and ironic emotion. It's why on those lists of fears you can have, people are more fearful about snakes than they are of dying. Fear is a short- and long-term emotion.

There are bad fear, less-bad fear, and good fear. I will explain in a moment but first, *bad fear* is obvious—it holds people back from taking the risks they need or it makes them take risks that are well beyond the reward. Bad fear forces us into bad decisions that we end up regretting later, like taking a job we know we don't want or staying in a dysfunctional relationship for too long. Bad fear talks down our confidence where we see everything as a glass half empty. Even the most confident and optimistic people have bad fears in them.

Corporate America is littered with stories of bad fears leading to bad decisions. In just the last few years, newspapers have headlined articles about Raj Rajaratnam, Bernie Madoff, Allen Stanford—guys who'd gone to jail for swindling innocent investors all for their own personal gain. Every time a story like that pops up you wonder, "Why?

Didn't they know they'd eventually be caught?" You wouldn't think fear is what motivated them to make billion dollar wagers that flouted the law. Surely these people have an arrogant and deceptive personality that is beyond normal, but deep down inside there is a great insecurity and fear. A fear of not mattering. A fear of losing to the other guy. A fear of being "less than." I'm no psychologist, but you only need to read their profiles and history to understand their core motivations. When Bernie Madoff finally confessed his sins for running the biggest Ponzi scheme in America, he said he suddenly felt at peace. He was no longer in fear of being caught, but he also was no longer fighting the fears that drove him to swindle thousands of investors. On Wall Street, there's a saying that fear and greed are the two driving forces in the stock markets. Both feed off each other, so if you can control those two emotions, you won't end up like a Bernie Madoff.

It's not just crooked Wall Street guys who succumb to bad fears. Sometimes, good guys make bad decisions based on bad fears. One such example is the merger of AOL with Time Warner in 2000 that has gone down in the annals of history as one of the worst transactions in modern business. The big motivator for Time Warner's chief executive, Gerald Levin, was that the online world was quickly encroaching upon his territory. Soon his magazines and television networks, including CNN, would be swallowed up by Internet companies. It's a fear that's come to fruition today so you could say that Gerry Levin was, in fact, quite ahead of his time.

But that fear led to a merger of two companies that never should have been combined in the first place. Bad blood began even before the contracts were signed. Thousands of people lost their jobs and retirement savings over the next few years. Eventually the two companies were separated again and AOL went from a lion in the media world to a deer in headlights.

Ted Turner, who was the largest single shareholder in AOL-Time Warner, lost the most money out of anyone. In a *New York Times* piece that ran on January 10, 2010, marking the 10-year anniversary of the deal, Turner said: "The Time Warner–AOL merger should pass into history like the Vietnam War and the Iraq and Afghanistan wars. It's one of the biggest disasters that have occurred to our country. I lost eighty percent of my worth and subsequently lost my job. We looked it up to see if I was the biggest loser of all time because I lost about $8 billion. But I don't think I was the biggest loser of all time. I think at one point Microsoft stock went down more than that for Bill Gates. I think he's the biggest winner and the biggest loser. I was in the top three or four of all time."

From that failure has come the beginnings of a comeback story. Tim Armstrong, the current AOL chief executive, remembers at the time watching the merger fiasco from the sidelines as a senior executive at Google. Eventually he was hired to turn around AOL.

"I think the first thing I did was I saw 9,000 out of the 10,000 people in person and flew around to tons of countries and visited all the offices. People asked one question: Do you think this company could be great again? I met with all the top customers, spent 100 days on the road, circled the world, and when I got back, I put up three whiteboards in New York. I wrote down what the employees said about our strategy, wrote down what the management team said, and I wrote down what I thought from listening to everyone. Pretty much everything was the same except I had one thing that was different. So there was an alignment between the employees and the customer base.

"So it started with the strategy and then after the strategy, we put the structure together and that changed the company. The second thing we did was work on morale. I put a policy in right away of employees first. I told employees that whether it was good or bad news, you'd hear it from me first. That was a big change. The last thing I did was I ripped down office walls, physically ripped them down, which by the way was the first thing I did. I did not know it would send the biggest cultural message but it did, that there was no difference here whether it was your first day on the job or you were the youngest person in the office, everything was open."

I asked Tim what he wrote down that was different from everyone else.

"I had put video down. We basically all had the same things—content, advertising, local—AOL services business but I had put down video." To Tim's vision, online video is now one of the fastest-growing parts of the Internet and mobile, and where advertising dollars are now headed.

I tell this story because it leads me to *good fear*. This kind of fear can be very motivating. It's the fear that we won't be able to live with ourselves if we don't move ahead. Good fear keeps us on the straight and narrow. Good fears are part of any successful comeback story, that after failure you dig inside yourself to come back better than you were before because of the fear that if you didn't, you wouldn't be able to live with yourself. Good fear, in general, is part of any success story.

Warren Buffett, the third-richest man in the world, agrees to multi-billion dollar deals on a handshake. When I mentioned that to him and said that was pretty fearless, he laughed.

"I'm not afraid of failure in financial matters."

"Why?" I ask.

"I just know that everything I do isn't going to work, but most of the things will and that's good enough. If I don't do anything, you know, my life would be pretty boring," he said. "And most of the time I'm going to be right but not all the time. So that means I'm not paralyzed by the fact that I might do something wrong. Everybody does something wrong."

"It sounds like you're more fearful of having an ordinary life," I observe.

"You know *that* would have been terrible. If I kept selling shirts at Penney's, that would not have been a happy life."

The good fear of having an ordinary life drove Buffett to accomplish extraordinary things in the financial world. He bought a small textile company called Berkshire Hathaway in the 1960s and turned it into one of the biggest conglomerates in the world, with over 70 companies under his watch and over $75 billion under management. He manages more than the economy of Syria. Buffett was also famous for his role in taking over the struggling Wall Street firm Salomon Brothers when it was swimming under a scandal brought upon by some rogue bond traders. At the time, Buffett had to testify in front of Congress and uttered the famous line that is replayed at every one of his annual meetings: "Lose money for the firm and I will be understanding, lose a shred of reputation for the firm and I will be ruthless."

Talk about instilling fear.

"Salomon, in the end, really started with two people when you get right down to it," Warren recalled. "The people that really caused the trouble were just a couple . . . it wasn't like you had 8,000 terrible people there.

"My main job then was to resolve the fact that four very important authorities like the Department of Justice and the U.S. Attorney, the [Federal] Reserve and the SEC, all wanted to see us go out of business, and so essentially I've got to say, 'Why take 8,000 people down because two people misbehaved?' I would try to find out all the problems that existed and come totally clean about everything that was wrong in the past. The future would be very much different if they would just give us a chance. So I was a good candidate to do that because I wasn't implicated in anything so I had nothing personally to worry about.

"There was one incident that people have long forgotten about, but after I had been there a little while, somebody made a mistake right before the close [of the stock market], and I don't know whether they added zeroes to an order . . . it was an honest mistake, but it looked like hell. It cost millions of dollars. And it looked like somebody at Salomon was playing games, but they weren't. And I told the people of Salomon, I said, 'I don't even want to know the name of that person, because as far as I'm concerned, he just made an honest mistake, and I'm not here to crucify guys for honest mistakes, I'm here to crucify anybody that does anything that tarnishes this firm in terms of intentional behavior.' So I sent the message out, basically I don't care who it was, it doesn't make any difference, we're just going to go to work tomorrow. I think it reinforced the message of what I expected and what I would tolerate."

When I tell Buffett he is pretty fearless, he says: "Yeah, but I was terrified of public speaking, for example. I took that Dale Carnegie course which changed my life in a big way. Just the other day . . . last week I was someplace and a woman came up to me and she said she had had the same experience, she had taken a Dale Carnegie course and it changed her life. I can't remember where I was. You don't have to worry about all your fears, but I'd certainly have a fear of being on *Dancing with the Stars* or something similar."

Which leads me to what I call *less-bad fears*. What do I mean by this? A less-bad fear is an almost good fear—a fear that's neither destructive nor overwhelmingly constructive. It can be both motivating and hindering. It's what I heard over and over again in my interviews, fears that were controllable, that helped people make the right decisions. It was . . . less bad than bad fears.

Chris Burch, the retail entrepreneur, describes his less-bad fear as a "fear of being unnoticed or fear of being not appreciated or loved or whatever because I was a terrible student."

"I've never had fear of losing a job. I've never reported to anyone. Until I lived through those experiences, until my Mom and Dad passed away, I didn't know the fear and pain of that happening. So I can't really put myself in other people's shoes on a fear of losing a job or fear of this."

When the economy was recovering from the devastation of the housing collapse, I heard again and again the phrase, "less bad." Economic data was less bad. The Federal Reserve, our central bank, was taking the less-bad approach, by putting money into the system to get the economy going. The creation of 45,000 jobs was less bad than losing jobs. It may not be good, but it's not bad. And for the last several years, this country has been forging ahead on less bad.

The key is to turn less bad into more good. I don't know how others do it but I know from the interviews and my own personal experience that one of the most helpful things is to just go through it and realize, *the world did not fall apart.*

Elon Musk mentioned that even when he was borrowing money to pay for rent because he had bet everything on his car company, he knew he would not be destitute. That is the same attitude people who seemingly have no fear embody—a rationalization that you can go through the thing you fear and still be okay. You have your health, family, and your mental capacity.

"Some years ago I spent time thinking about the moves I made, what my downside was," said Sallie Krawcheck, the prominent Wall Street investment banker. "So my first big promotion, which was then director of research at Bernstein, I thought, well, gee, if I failed, what's my downside? My downside is I'll go back to being a research analyst. Okay. That's not so bad, actually, I loved the job. It will be a little embarrassing for a period of time, because you failed. When Sandy Weill brought me over to Citigroup, in a very public move, I went from managing 386 people on a Tuesday to 20,000 on a Wednesday, and I thought, okay, what's my downside? Well, my downside is I'm probably fired. Okay. I can deal with that, right? To have the ability to have this life experience, some people would say, 'Oh, my God. I could get fired.' Could be. *Could be.* That's how it worked for me. For me, getting publically fired and being in the newspapers, while not a lot of fun, you know, is livable. I can live through that. And you've seen all the research that says people on their deathbed regret what they haven't done, not what they have done."

"The unknown is more fearful than the known and a lot of people don't think through failure like they think through their success," said Nolan Bushnell, who saw several of his companies rise and fall, including Atari. "If I fail, what does that failure look like? Does it mean I don't sell enough? Does it mean I lose payroll? You have to run through logical conclusions."

When I asked Nolan what he considered his biggest failure, he said definitively: "Robots."

"I fell in love with personal robots in 1983. I couldn't get investors to believe in it, and so I spent a huge amount of my own money. But the investors were right. I lost a lot of money. My robot company represented the single biggest financial loss in my business career. I lost over 20 million bucks at a time when $20 million was worth a lot more than today. If you really look failure in the eye and really think it through, step by step, very seldom do you lose the house, the car, almost never the car. You can go flat out bankrupt, but most of the time, you can work out payment schedules with your creditors. You'll have a couple of bad years, years where you don't go to Hawaii, your kids go to public school, but that's it."

Susan Lyne said her career is littered with mistakes—bright ideas that failed to make money.

"One mistake that I've made more than once is believing because I love an idea, that it's a business," she said. "And just not listening hard enough to the doubts. The passion for the product blinded me to the challenges. Gilt Taste was a project I absolutely adored. I was completely convinced because we had a great team, a great product, that we were going to win with this. I just didn't look hard enough at the things that were challenging about it, including the fact that it was all drop shipped so that if you put more than one thing into your cart, you're going to have multiple shipping charges. The sticker shock of shipping that way adds up to 30 to 40 percent of the cost of your basket. That's just not acceptable.

"I made the same mistake with *Blueprint Magazine* with Martha Stewart. I thought the idea of doing a younger women's version of

DIY with great taste and great photography was a cool idea, but I looked at the extremely optimistic view of how much cash we were going to burn on it. It was a mistake. You should look at the worst case projections and make sure you're comfortable with that cash burn."

In the end, what is the difference between good fear, less-bad fear, and bad fear? Not much other than *what you do with it*. If you wallow in the bad fear, it will destroy your self-confidence and worth. It will make your life much less.

More recently, I faced those fears when I was struggling with whether I would make the switch into television. Right now, the switch seems so natural but back then, friends, colleagues, and associates were all telling me how difficult it would be to make the transition from newspaper reporter to television reporter.

For one, I'd be competing with people who had years of experience already. I had never read or written a script, much less reported live for a television station. People think you can just stand in front of a camera and talk, but being able to be cogent, live, and on point in the heat of the moment requires more skill than the ability to just talk.

Second, I was making a nice living as a newspaper reporter. I was gaining a reputation as a pretty good writer and business reporter, having broken a few stories for the *Financial Times* and contributed to or led on some big feature pieces. I may not have been making the millions but compared to my friends in the same field, I was driving a nice car, living in a comfy home, and doing interesting work. I had my eyes set on the *New York Times* or another large, national publication. So did my journalist friends. In fact, many of them have ended up at the national newspapers like the *Wall Street Journal* and *Washington Post*.

Third, I was hitting 30 and thinking about children. Already many of my friends were pregnant. I was worried if I waited too long, the timing would not be right. But then the timing could not have been worse either. I couldn't understand why I had two desires in my gut at the same time—to both switch into a new career and have a baby.

All these thoughts swam in my head for a while and the fear of moving on one but not the other only paralyzed me. On one weekend, we spent the day with my family in Ocean City, by the Jersey shore. We were sitting in our beach house relaxing when my father could see I was lost in my head.

"What's wrong? What's bothering you?"

I told him I was just confused. Starting a family is a huge commitment. And then to try to do that while also looking to switch careers is another big commitment. Not to mention worrying about finding a job and your finances.

I'm not sure exactly what my father said, but he helped crystallize it for me. I think it was more the fact that *he* said it rather than the exact words that hit me. Here was my father, a man who wanted me to always go the safe route in my career, telling me to take a risk. Just go for it, he advised, and let the future work itself out.

"Do both and see what happens."

In that moment, what had been a set of bad and less-bad fears turned into good fear—I began to fear the consequences of not going for it more than doing it. I thought to myself, if in five years, I was in the same spot as I was now, would I be happy? And the answer was an unequivocal no. There was no turning back.

Last time I checked, we only have one life. Your job is to get rid of the bad fear and turn the less-bad fear into good fear that motivates you to strive for the bigger.

Chapter 7

Finances

I call this chapter "Finances," but it's really about "Money."

Money is the exchange of one item for another at a *predeter-mined* value. We could exchange anything as money—a piece of grass, a glass marble, or in the generally accepted case, a piece of a paper or metal coin. A dollar really is worth $0.04 when you get down to its basic cost. But a dollar is valued at a dollar because in our global exchange system, when we compare it to other currencies, the dollar has a value that is determined each and every second against all other currencies. In trader talk, a dollar is always valued at what it's worth against something else—the dollar against the Japanese yen, the dollar against the European euro, the dollar against the Australian dollar. The same is true on the flip side—the Japanese yen against the dollar, the Australian dollar against the U.S. dollar. So you could say, the dollar is always competing with other countries. So far, we're still the strongest guy in the gym—nobody else quite matches in breadth and muscle.

People use the dollar—or lots of dollars—to compete. As the saying goes, "Money is the way to keep score." I heard Sam Zell quote this but I also heard it from many successful people for years. Sometimes people keep score with big houses, perfect kids, and job titles but the ultimate benchmark is money. And it doesn't matter if you have a lot of money. Someone always has more. I have sat down with people who have hundreds of millions of dollars to their name and they feel inferior to the successful businessmen who have more than a billion to theirs. Around this time, one billionaire, Brazilian oil magnate Eike Batista, was making news for exactly the wrong reason: losing tons of money. Learning the hard way to abide by the "shut up while you're ahead" school, Batista once declared he was going to be the richest man in the world, beating Warren Buffett, Bill Gates, and Mexican telecom tycoon Carlos Slim. It was as if God heard his obnoxious boast and like in the Book of Job, started to strip Batista of all his wealth. By July 2013, Batista stopped being a billionaire.

You can't knock the guy for having the gumption. Most people who earn more money end up fearing the loss of it. It's difficult to feel sorry for a millionaire or billionaire but it is, as research shows, a peculiar circumstance that money creates more instability and fear than it cures. Friends constantly ask you to invest in their bright ideas or to borrow money. Sons and daughters suspect others want to be with them only for their wealth. Someone is always after you to undermine your business. With greater wealth comes greater responsibility— homes to take care of, bigger bills, staff, and constant efforts to keep up appearances. For the ultra-rich like Bill Gates, you can get away with looking like the middle-aged dad picking up eggs at the supermarket, but for others who are getting wealthier, you want to show it off with bigger cars, houses, nicer clothes, fantastic vacations. You're on the classic "hedonic treadmill" where you're running faster just to stay in the same place.

The *New York Times* ran a Sunday opinion piece in March 2013 by a tech millionaire who jumped off the treadmill and sold all his belongings to live in a 420-square-foot apartment in Manhattan. "For me, it took fifteen years, a great love, and a lot of travel to get rid of all the inessential things I had collected and live a bigger, better, richer life with less," Graham Hill wrote.

On the flip side, you have those who are peering up like fish from the bottom of a tank, watching someone like Hill and saying, "Wait a minute, I live in a 420-square-foot space and I would rather be *you* as a millionaire. When am I going to get there? How?" You're loaded with debt, working two jobs, you want to start a family but it's too expensive. You feel stuck in a lifestyle rut. You want to save but you can hardly get by on your paychecks with the rent/mortgage so high, the car payments, the babysitting costs; or you're earning a decent salary but not anything big that you can build a gigantic retirement egg on. It can seem like once you get rich, then you'll be happy and life will be good. Why do you think so many people play the lottery or get duped into get-rich quick schemes?

Research, for the most part, shows that money *does not* buy happiness. Back in the 1970s, a University of Southern California professor named Richard Easterlin came up with the Easterlin Paradox. The basic research behind this is that at some point, once basic needs are met, more money does not buy more happiness. He observed data from the 1940s through the 1970s and found that while people's incomes rose, their happiness did not. In time, his research has been challenged by other academics who say there's no cutoff point—that in fact, for some people, more money does mean more happiness.

But it's not difficult to see where Easterlin was coming from. Other happiness indexes have come out that show that if we're the richest country in the world, we're sure a bunch of miserable people. According to the 2012 Happy Planet Index put together by the New Economics Foundation, out of 151 countries, Costa Rica, Vietnam, and Colombia are the top three happiest countries. The United States is 105. The latest Organisation for Economic Co-operation and Development (OECD) Life Satisfaction Survey found that Switzerland, Norway, and Iceland were the top three most satisfied countries. The United States was number 14.

All of this is to say that if you are looking for money to buy you happiness, you're in it for the wrong reasons. Maybe some million-aires have to sell off all their possessions to understand that. But *you* don't. It's not shameful to want to make money. As Warren Buffett said, "There's nothing wrong with loving the money.

"But if you're kind of a phony to start with, you're going to be a bigger phony when you make a lot of money. And if you're kind of mean, you can get meaner as you make money," Warren said. "But if you're generous, you get more generous. I think money and age both tend to push you further and further into the direction in which you start. There are exceptions to that, but I think that's generally true."

Money will make you only more of who you are. If you're a miserable person and poor and you strike it rich, you'll simply be miserable and rich. If you're happy and poor, you'll be happy and rich. It is almost a universal axiom that the people who get rich by scheming their way to the top will see their fortunes fall just as fast; that people who pursue their careers with the only goal of getting the six-figure salary will inevitably squander it all away or suffer in other ways. It may not be Easterlin's Paradox but it's a paradox all its own.

★★★★★★★★★

Now that we know money can't buy happiness, what can it buy?

It buys us better health care.
It buys us better education.
It buys us freedom.

This last one is extremely important.

As we found out before, Bob Benmosche, the CEO of AIG, is someone who speaks his mind. He isn't afraid of many people. He can say "F—you" to people and walk off the job. He has the guts to do that because he has the financial freedom. And that didn't begin when he made a lot of money. As Bob told me, that thinking began when he had nothing.

"For me it's very simple: to make sure that I have plenty of money and that I can afford the things I want and I never go back," he said. "My Dad died when I was 10. My mother was left with $250,000 of debt and she had four children. My sister was 12, I was 10, I had a sister, 5, and a brother, 3. To be finding yourself without a will, without insurance, and $250,000 of debt . . . if that were to happen today it would be tough, but it happened in 1954.

"My father was a photographer. He did a man-on-the-street column in the paper to make some extra money. They loved it—little man-in-the-street pictures. It was at the local newspaper in Monticello,

New York, in Sullivan County. Originally we were from Brooklyn. [My father] bought some cabins and a restaurant and a bar. He wanted to run that business. Then he got this idea that he should build motels, not out of town but in town, so people could walk around and do things in the village.

"So he put that idea to work in 1952 to 1953 and he built a motel right in the middle of Monticello, New York, in the Catskills. The only problem was he didn't have any money. So everybody was so intrigued with his idea that lumber companies sent lumber and the plumbers sent plumbing supplies and everything was fine except when he finished the project in December of 1954, he realized that there was no business because the season was over. He had no money and no visible financing and at 50 years old, he died of a heart attack. So it literally killed him."

"He didn't borrow the money? He couldn't ask people for time to pay them back?" I asked.

"He didn't borrow money, he just owed money to all the suppliers, because they all loved him, they trusted him, he's a bright guy. And so I learned at ten years old . . . what risks you run in terms of foreclosures. My mother used to start her day at six in the morning. She used to get us off to school, the two older ones, took care of the two younger ones; managed to keep an eye on the new motel which was in Monticello Village . . . and she took care of the restaurant. She made sure the cabins were clean and she made sure that the bar was well covered . . . and she closed the bar some time around one in the morning. And she did that day in and day out, except Sunday."

"I have to speak to Alfred University's graduating class in upstate New York, where I graduated from. I'm doing the commencement address . . . the big CEO from AIG," he continued with a smirk on his face, clearly bemused by his status. "I usually talk about things that I think are kind of practical and kind of direct—that's my approach to things. And it worried me a little bit that they're going to say, well, okay, so he was the CEO of MetLife and he is the CEO of AIG and way beyond my reach, so why even bother listening?

"So what I said to myself was, maybe they need to understand that I didn't start out as a CEO, and that how I started my life was, you know, it would have been nice if it were different, and it would have been nice if my Dad had life insurance. It would have been nice if he had a good bank loan. That would have made it easier on all of us to figure out how to run these businesses. But he didn't. And my first rule in my own life is deal with the hand that's been dealt you."

Later on, Bob let on to his second rule that was born from the first.

"You have to decide what's enough. And you have to make sure that you have enough. I call it 'f— you' money. Screw you money."

"F— you money?" I repeated.

"You don't want to be beholden to anybody in your career. You want to be able to come to work every day and be able to feel free to make the judgment that you want to make. And throughout my career that's been very helpful because I knew that I was doing things that I could be shot for, but I didn't care. You've got to start with the confidence to know if it's not what you want and you can't believe in what you're doing, you have the freedom to find something different."

Bob's father did not have f— you money—he was drowning in IOUs and the stress directly killed him. So the son who watched his father held hostage to money made it his core mission in life to ensure money did not hold a gun to his head.

"What I've done through my life is to say I don't need to have the newest car, I don't have to have the newest fancy watch. I got this watch twenty to twenty-five years ago," Bob said, lifting his arm to show me. "It's a Cartier. It's a very nice watch. And everybody says, 'Oh, I saw a beautiful this and a beautiful that, and I'm going to buy this watch and that watch . . .' and I said, 'You know what? I like this watch. I don't need the fancy watches anymore.' At one time, you wanted somebody to recognize you're doing well. And throughout my life I've always been able to say I need the freedom more than I need the fancy suit. I need the freedom more than the fancy shoes. I need the freedom more than the fancy car. And so in 1984 I didn't have any debt and I haven't had debt since."

Having that financial freedom means knowing what at the core will make you satisfied. Is there a number? Is there a quantity? Is it okay to have a goal that keeps moving higher? A survey by the Swiss financial firm UBS found that a majority of millionaires felt having at least $5 million was considered wealthy.

How did they define wealthy?

"Investors define wealth as not having financial constraints on their activities," said the report. In other words, being able to have f— you money.

But is $5 million the magic number to feel secure? A fascinating study done by Boston College's Center on Wealth and Philanthropy found the wealthier you get, the more you need to feel secure. Researchers asked an elite group of the ultra-wealthy in the United States to talk about what it's really like to be rich and, perhaps to no one's great surprise, a majority of them felt very insecure about their financial situation. As described in a 2011 *Atlantic* article, many of them felt they needed to have 25 percent more in the bank to feel really secure. One respondent said unless he had $1 billion in the bank, he wouldn't feel secure. Read that last line again: Unless he had $1 billion—enough to buy *five* Boeing Dreamliner airplanes—this one individual would not feel safe.

I asked Sam Zell what it was like to be rich. Does something change when you get to the level of a billionaire?

"I'm sure it does for each person. For me, I don't know what anything costs. Literally, I do not know what anything costs."

"Like a bottle of water?" I asked.

"Yeah, I mean, I know and hear it's $3 or $2 but I don't know. I don't buy anything. If I need something, somebody gets it for me. So in that respect, I'm distanced from what you might call the day-to-day reality of money. And I think that certainly if I had ever lived under a tight budget I'd be much better able to answer your question, but I've also lived very parsimoniously. I have a plane and an apartment in New York [but] I'm still wearing the same jeans I wore when I was fourteen! [*Laughter*] It has a lot to do with my own attitudes, which are that everybody has to be who they are. I have to be who I am and that doesn't change. I've spent my whole life going right when everybody else went left."

Sam went on to describe what can only be categorized as a rich person's dilemma—how to really spend all that money wisely. "I'm spending a significant amount of my time on charitable stuff. But not on the boards; I don't sit on any nonprofit boards. I don't do that kind of stuff. Another thing I don't do is give money to an organization just to get my name on a building. I say, 'Let's create programs that can make a difference.'"

Sam has spent the last few years funding programs for the creative arts at the University of Michigan and entrepreneurs at Northwestern University, and minting new real estate developers at the Wharton School at the University of Pennsylvania. He mentioned one of his greatest achievements started thirteen years ago in Israel where he helped create an incubator program for new companies.

"The best part of the story is the graduates of this program are now the number one choice for employment by anybody in Israel," he said. "They call themselves 'The Zell-ots.' That's really terrific—that you can actually create that kind of environment."

****

So what is f— you money?

The answer is . . . it depends. It's frustrating not to have a one-size-fits-all answer but, as you can see, f— you money is a moving target. Some people feel it's six months' worth of wages. Others wouldn't feel comfortable unless they had a year's worth of income socked away in their accounts. My goal has always been to save ten percent of what I earned before taxes, which some years I've achieved and others I haven't. I'm not always so sure *that* high a percentage is a good thing because it's been a mental barrier to putting that cash to use. There's security . . . and then there's hoarding your cash like a squirrel hoarding nuts. Provided, of course, you have cash to hoard.

Having the cash is the same as buying your freedom. It allows you to have the peace of mind that if something were to happen, you could walk away. If you looked at it that way, the money you accumulate becomes an empowering tool that allows you to pursue the things you want. Some people save money as an outgrowth of their fear—they *need* this money in case they get fired or laid off. There is nothing wrong with saving the money, but rather than look at it as a cushion for a negative event, look at it as a springboard for the future. In your mind, you want to think: I will have a certain amount of money so I can have the freedom to make the choices I need to make to get to my ultimate goals. The f— you money is your independence.

If money buys you freedom, then why not make lots of it?

Americans have a love/hate relationship with money. We are both embarrassed by vapid displays of wealth and admirers of the very rich (see: folk-hero status of Warren Buffett). When someone takes a job to just get rich, we cringe. Talking about your salary or your possessions is distasteful and obnoxious. Americans want to feel that whoever is rich got there for a nobler cause than enriching himself or herself, which is why the stereotype of the predatory Wall Street investment banker is so hated (see: Gordon Gekko). Around the time of this writing, two "bad guys" of Wall Street were thrust into the national spotlight—the young, brash executive named Fabrice Tourre who helped Goldman Sachs package those smelly housing-related securities, and Steve Cohen, the balding hedge fund billionaire whose traders were accused of making some smelly inside trades. It didn't seem to make a huge difference to the public that Steve himself had not been charged with any wrongdoing. Every time an article was written about Cohen, there was mention made of his predilection for fine art by Pablo Picasso, Willem de Kooning, and Jasper Johns, the purpose of which was to not only underscore his wealth, but to contrast the beauty against the beast.

In Asia, or particularly, in Hong Kong and China, money is viewed in a slightly different way. Everybody is hustling to make more money. I try not to generalize but I've lived off and on in Hong Kong, China, and Taiwan for the better part of two decades and I can say it's pretty prevalent. People who take jobs to "help people" are considered a little strange.

When I lived in Taiwan, my aunt came to visit me one night.

"How much is this flat?"

"How much money do you make?"

"What did this washing machine cost?"

The questions were endless. She didn't mean to be rude but it was perfectly normal to ask questions about money, especially of a family member. Money is a way to buy freedom and in some cultures, it's the *only* way to buy freedom.

In the United States, business news is separate from general news. In Hong Kong, business news *is* general news. It's not uncommon to see stories about property prices leading newscasts alongside the latest crime reports. Press conferences held by the city's tycoons are covered like presidential briefings—they are must-see TV. My Chinese colleagues were always hustling to make more money. One was setting up a photography business. Another was opening a spa. Yet another was looking for a rich husband, just like her girlfriends. At another time, when a friend and I went off to Mongolia to backpack along the countryside, I got strange looks. Backpacking around the world is such

an idealistic Western custom; the Chinese have no time for such trivi-
alities. They want to make money and they want to make it now.

Back in the United States, making money is not a bad thing but it
shouldn't be the *only* thing. I heard that repeatedly in my interviews with
CEOs. It's cliche yes, but it's one of those cliches that happens to be true.

Jamie Dimon, the CEO of JPMorgan, said: "It cannot just be about
the money. I've seen so many people, if they don't get more money or
a bigger title at the next job they don't want to do it. But that's not
how careers work. If you want to broaden out and learn, you're going
to have to move around and sideways sometimes."

And as if to illustrate the complex relationship people have with
money, he added: "How many times have we seen people who pound
the table here for money and they'll take a job for half somewhere
else? It's about quality of life, feeling respected, and growing." The
point being that the pursuit of more money isn't always about the cold,
hard cash; it's about power, control, freedom, and pride. Warren Buffett
has said repeatedly that he tap dances to work. "I mean, if you get to be
my age, or even sixty or seventy, and you have a fair number of people
who you love and who love you, you're going to be a happy person.
And then on top of that if you've got a job you love. . . . I'm very fortunate. Most people have to retire at sixty-five or something like that
and I get to continue what I enjoy doing more than anything else."

Even the legendary anti–establishment singer Bob Dylan understood the definition of a successful life: "What's money? A man is a
success if he gets up in the morning and goes to bed at night and in
between does what he wants to do."

★★★★★★★★

I have purposely tried not to make this chapter about personal finance.

There is nothing wrong with personal finance. My first book, *Age
Smart*, covered aspects of personal finance. But I sometimes wonder if
the Department of Education required every student to take account-
ing or finance courses in school, perhaps we wouldn't need so many
financial planning books and websites. Many times I've heard successful
people, especially women, say they wished they'd learned how to read
a balance sheet at a young age. A majority of us do not know what to
do with our money, whether we have a lot or a little of it. The problem

is very basic: It's really hard to earn money but it's just so damn easy to spend it.

The reason why I have not wanted to talk about personal finance is because there are already vast amounts of information on the subject.

Despite the enormous amount of data and information, the rules of personal finance, from what I can observe, boil down to five basic ingredients:

1. Minimize debt.
2. Better to own versus rent (eventually).
3. Save early and invest.
4. Diversify your money into stocks, bonds, property, and other assets.
5. Buy insurance (medical, dental, car) and update your will regularly.

These are all sensible recommendations and if you pick up any personal finance book, it will incorporate one or all of these.

The issue is something Chris Burch, the retail CEO, said at the end of our conversation when he lashed out at one particular personal finance book author: "I find it very defeatist, very much hold onto your money and don't do this. Creating more f—ing fear . . . why do you want to make everyone go to bed at night and worry to death?"

What people really should be going to bed doing, as Chris would point out, is dreaming up ways to make more money and becoming more valuable. Far too much energy, he says, is placed on protecting your assets and not enough on how to grow them, whether that asset is actual cash or yourself. Entrepreneurs understand this like second nature but for others, the idea is frightening. If it weren't frightening, all of us would be entrepreneurs. But as we know, only 15 percent of us think we actually have what it takes to strike out on our own.

Gary Vaynerchuk calls it "smurfing it up." He is a venture capitalist who began by inheriting his father's wine business in New Jersey, then sweated it out on stage years ago at a Web 2.0 Expo conference telling people they needed to keep adding value to themselves.

"Look yourself in the mirror and ask yourself 'What do I want to do every day for the rest of my life?' Do that! I promise you can monetize that shit. If you love Alf, do an Alf blog. You collect Smurfs? *Smurf it up!* Whatever you need to do, do it!"

But does smurfing it up always mean starting a business? No. It simply means adding value to yourself, whether it be learning a new skill that makes you more attractive to an employer or going back to school to broaden your area of expertise. It means networking with people and opening yourself to new thoughts and ideas that could spark an interest, an invention, a new career. Making more money is in direct correlation to how much more valuable you are—what the sum of your skills, learning, and expertise can bring in the marketplace.

Jeff Hayzlett, who knows a thing or two about making brands valuable as the former chief marketing officer at Kodak, said he thinks of himself as a company. (Again, the brand of one concept.) Every 18 months, he told me, has to involve a new "activation"—a new book, new show, or new project that shows he's adding value to the marketplace. Just 12 months ago he signed onto Bloomberg TV as a contributor.

"Always think: How can you activate on your career?" he said.

When you think about it, companies have to be the same way to grow. Every year, customers expect Apple to come out with another iPhone or iPad, another activation as Jeff would call it. If Apple doesn't, people say the company has lost its edge, making it easier for competitors like Google and Samsung to march further into its turf. Fast food restaurants like McDonald's have to come out with a fresh, new food item regularly so people think the company is young, hip, and relevant. Think of the Mighty Wings and the McWrap. Fashion designers have to come out with new looks every season in the hopes they'll create the most buzz for their label. If you're not doing something to add value to your career on a regular basis, you're going to languish. It doesn't matter if you're a nurse, teacher, salesman, or mechanic. It can be something as simple as taking a class to increase your knowledge or joining a networking group related to your profession and volunteering for a position. Anything that helps you *grow* counts.

So I could easily see where Jeff was coming from. But how does that relate to where Chris was coming from, lamenting that too many people are worried to death about their money?

For some proof, I only needed to look at the stock market. As of June 2013, about $10 trillion was still sitting on the benches, either in certificates of deposit, money market funds, or plain old bank accounts.

That means the money was earning nearly nothing in interest. That is a signal that the average investor is scared to put money into the stock market. Because of that fear, if you stayed out of the market since 2008, when the recession bottomed, you would have missed out on 95 percent in returns. That means if you had put $10,000 in the stock market in December 2008, you would be richer by $9,500—almost doubling your money.

But that's the point—a good many of us are afraid to invest our money. That same fear of financial loss is also what prevents us from branching out and pursuing our entrepreneurial dreams. We're afraid to lose our money and our security. That's where Chris and Jeff meet. They're both saying the same thing. While many books out there teach us how to get out of debt and invest wisely, Chris and Jeff are saying we are all focused on the wrong thing. Investing in your 401(k) is *not* going to get you rich—it might give you a comfortable life if you do it well but it won't make you wealthy. Focus first on your career and yourself, how *you* can increase your value, and the money will follow. Be *proactive* about making money first, not *reactive* about keeping it.

Which is not to say that being sensible with your money is a bad thing. It's clearly good practice. But as Sam Zell would say, it's "cold-cock simple." Always make sure you spend less than you make and invest your money in a variety of different ways—real estate, stocks, and bonds. With that formula, you're almost always assured financial security. I've always believed personal finance is a lot like dieting. There really is no magic formula. Dieting is all about calories in and calories out, supplemented by exercise. There's variance within but if you strictly want to lose weight, you eat less than you burn and watch your waistline narrow.

Managing your finances is exactly the same way. You spend less than you earn and save the rest. You put that money into investments and hope it grows and continue to invest even when the economy hits a rough patch. Eventually, you'll turn out better off than you were before you started.

Once you clear that hurdle in your head, you can focus more on what really matters, which is growing your career. That's certainly a far better subject to fall asleep to than worrying about your 401(k).

Chapter 8

Flow

The man who created the pioneering video game company Atari prefers to play old-fashioned chess.

When Nolan Bushnell got on the phone with me, that was the first thing he said: "When I play chess, I have a complete tree of moves, five or six moves in advance. For any move [my opponent] makes, I've thought through that move for three, four more moves. So if I wanted to, I could immediately move after he moves. Now if you move fast, I move fast, then he moves fast and then we stop and recalculate. I play all-in about an hour a day."

Nolan is describing something that happens to him when he plays chess that also happens to millions of teenagers who play video games. They get in the *flow*. Flow is a term first coined by a Hungarian psychologist, Mihaly Csikszentmihalyi, who described it simply as the moment when a person is completely immersed in what they are doing. I can say that in various moments of writing this book, I have been in the flow. You lose track of time. Your world is narrowed into the task at hand and in my case, it was translating my thoughts onto the computer screen.

Mihaly studied many people who easily slip into the flow—composers, artists, and athletes. But everybody enjoys a state of flow, whether it's gardening, cycling, or writing. Even companies enjoy a state of flow. Sometimes you can feel the energy of a company that's on a core mission, like Apple. Apple under Steve Jobs had a flow. So does Starbucks under Howard Schultz. Flow is not only being in the moment, but enjoying the moment for what it is and nothing more.

I usually joke on my program that I loved playing video games. The truth is, I really did. It wasn't until years later I realized why I enjoyed it so much, even though I know how geeky and unfeminine it makes me sound.

I distinctly—and embarrassingly—remember weekends where a new game would come out and I would park myself in front of the television with friends and we would play all day into the night with food as a side concern (remember, I was just out of college). At the end of the night, you'd feel a little greasy and gross, like an addict coming off a high, and vow you'd never play that way again until the next day when you'd be itching to turn the game on. It wasn't until I conquered *Metal Gear Solid* that I felt I could kick the habit.

Part of the reason why video games are so addicting is they encourage flow—a state where you are rewarded for your intensity and concentration. Each win kicks you up to a new level where more challenges await, challenges that are just difficult enough to keep you going back for more. If the challenges were too easy, you'd easily fall out of flow and lose interest. If the challenges were too hard, you'd eventually get angry, throw the controller at the television set and eat the rest of your pizza pie.

Money may not buy you happiness, but in many cases, flow does. When people encourage you to follow your passions, what they're saying is follow what gives you flow. What feels like you "want to do" versus you "have to do." People grow bored with their jobs for a variety of reasons and one of them is a lack of flow. Flipping burgers at McDonald's might be challenging in the first few weeks (I've tried it, and it's not that easy to make a cheeseburger in 30 seconds or less), but after you've mastered the skill, workers ask, what's next? What can I do to move up the ladder and grab more challenges?

According to the U.S. Bureau of Labor Statistics, about 2 million Americans quit their jobs every month. That's an astounding number of people who leave—almost 16 percent of the people who are currently looking for a job. So any boss who thinks that just because the job market is tight, his or her staff won't leave is dangerously underestimating the power of the pursuit of happiness. A Harris Interactive Poll found three-quarters of people working right now would jump ship if they could. About a third were already actively looking for a new job. Among the top reasons for leaving a job were because they hated their bosses, office politics, and a lack of empowerment or recognition, according an Accenture report.

Jimmy Lee's "Killer" Workout

Several successful A-type executives I spoke with mentioned starting off their mornings with an early workout. The workout gets the blood flowing and the brain humming.

Jimmy Lee offers another kind of workout that is just as effective for your career—and you don't have to sweat so much. During the course of our interview, Jimmy pulled out a sheet of paper that outlines his "killer work-habit" workout that in typical Jimmy style, is long, blunt, detailed, and colorful.

I pulled out a few of my favorites from the 25 he listed because they drive home some of the *Work Smarts* points:

- **Ask questions:** Never be embarrassed to raise your hand and ask a question when you don't understand something—that's how you learn. Whatever the question, chances are you aren't the first and won't be the last to ask it.
- **Don't guess:** If someone asks a question, never begin your answer with, "I think . . ." Know the answer and deliver it with confidence. If you don't know the answer, be upfront and ask for time to find it.
- **Look sharp:** Dress for the job you want. Your appearance is the first thing people notice, and always looking your best shows that you respect your work and your clients.
- **Being on time is being late:** If you wait until you get to your desk in the morning to start thinking about the day ahead, it's already too late.

> • **Prepare like a demon:** There's no such thing as being over-prepared. Do your homework. Being prepared for anything and everything will give you increased confidence and make you unflappable.

Does flow cure that unhappiness? Not in all cases, but it helps tremendously if you love what you do and doing it rewards you. I always say some of the best days on our show are when we've had a particularly fast-paced two hours with news-making guests and a lot of breaking news and suddenly, instead of us all working in disparate parts, we come together with one mind and put on a seamless program for the viewer. It doesn't matter if we get the accolades after but for our team, knowing we put on a great program is enough for us.

A common refrain I'll utter during that time is, "Wow, it didn't feel like two hours." That's what happens in flow. You almost kick into autopilot. Everything is working so well you lose track of time.

At another level, high-performing athletes describe flow as something clicking and suddenly, they're just on. The Brazilian Formula One driver Ayrton Senna, perhaps the greatest racer of all time before his career ended in a fiery crash, described flow this way: "And suddenly I realized that I was no longer driving the car consciously. I was driving it by a kind of instinct, only I was in a different dimension."

★★★★★★★★

Sometimes people describe flow as "enjoying the moment."

Behavioral psychologists will tell you that the more times you can enjoy a moment, whether it's a half hour in the gym, going for a long walk, or sitting on a beach looking at the water, the more happy you'll be. Some people wake up every morning and meditate. Others do yoga at lunchtime. In a *Yoga Journal* article, Bill Gross, the manager of the world's largest bond fund, Pimco, said he does yoga every morning.

"Some of my best ideas come during Sirsasana [translation: Headstand]," Gross said in the piece. After the session is over, "a light bulb turns on, and I'm on to something."

Warren Buffett similarly talked about his light-bulb moment while relaxing in his bathtub, when he came up with the idea to invest $5 billion in Bank of America in 2011. That led to numerous recountings of other prominent people who'd taken to their bathtubs for bright ideas, including former Federal Reserve Chairman Alan Greenspan who wrote his memoir while sitting in a bathtub.

The more people enjoy the moment, the happier they are. These people are usually optimists. They're the glass-half-full people who see a world of possibilities simply because they see the world for what it is at the moment. Vicky Schiff is one of those people. She's a real estate investor who I met through another friend, who, by the way, is also into the flow theory. Optimists tend to attract other optimists.

When Vicky came by my office, she was taking pictures of our Bloomberg office building. "Wow, it's just so beautiful," she said looking around. Of course I walk in and out of the building every day seeing nothing but the thoughts in my head. She carried bags full of toys for her son from FAO Schwartz and immediately I felt a little pang of guilt—I work only a few blocks away from the store and never find time to pop in for my kids, except at Christmas.

Vicky summed up her view on life from a movie line.

"Remember *Joe Versus the Volcano*?" she asked. "Remember what Meg Ryan's character said? I feel exactly the same way. I can't understand how people don't appreciate what's around them. Luck comes along every minute."

Later I looked up the exact quote.

"My father says that almost the whole world is asleep," Meg Ryan's character, Patricia, says. "Everybody you know. Everybody you see. Everybody you talk to. He says that only a few people are awake and they live in a state of constant total amazement."

****

Like many things in this book, how to achieve flow is pretty simple. Most things should not be overthought and flow most of all.

How to achieve flow begins with *finding what you love doing*. What would you do whether you were paid for it or not? What activity can you immerse yourself in, whether reading, writing poetry, or cooking? Sometimes, it's doing nothing but sitting there, enjoying the world around you.

"I find that foreign travel is very, very good for ideas, this combination of struggling with the new, maybe trying to speak a different language, and then having leisure at the same time," Nolan said. "I used to love to sit down in a Paris café, drinking coffee, watching the world go by and jotting ideas in my notebook."

Getting to flow also means *setting aside time for it*. Bill Gross spends every morning doing yoga. Others hit the gym before work. Some tinker with their cars. Others garden. Whatever the case, you have to set aside time to get in the flow.

One thing to remember: There's usually *a goal at the end*. Flow is about being in the moment but that moment begins with a goal. My goal is to finish this book. A person at the gym is looking to complete a workout routine. At work, a goal might be to finish a marketing presentation. The path towards the goal is the flow but that flow has to find its finish.

Part Three

Postcards from the C-Suite

Chapter 9

What It's Really Like to Be a CEO

A businessman said to me the other day that it's more difficult to become a Fortune 50 CEO than it is to become a professional athlete. He said: "It's harder to get to the top of the corporate ladder than it is to be an elite athlete. Isn't that something?"

I never thought of it that way but the more those words sank in, the more I realized he was right. Getting to what's called the C-suite—the uppermost level of management—is a competition just like in any other sport. And like a game, there's only one winner in the end. Jim Reynolds, the CEO of the boutique investment bank Loop Capital, is friends with many professional athletes around Chicago—former Super Bowl champs, basketball stars, golf pros.

"Each and every one of these professional athletes is an entrepreneur. Their company is themselves and their body. Once that body breaks down, it's over," he said. "When you're a young athlete with

117

quickness and speed, raw physical prowess, you learn about how to do things and how not to exert yourself so much, learn how to anticipate the plays better and read the other guys' eyes. CEOs are the same way—they have to be on top of their game, every game. And there are hundreds of people looking to take Kobe Bryant's spot, or LeBron James'. At the point you stop or cease growing as a professional athlete, then that's the point you open yourself to be susceptible to the competition. You need to make sure you're mentally at the top of the game . . . as a CEO you have to learn the plays of your competitors, what's the next pop in the market. I draw many parallels between elite athletes and very good CEOs and entrepreneurs—when you think about it, the differences are almost imperceptible. You're doing different things but mentally the strategies are very close."

In fact, as I learned quite quickly, you do need to be physically fit to be a CEO.

"The physical part of it is the hardest—it just *mounts*," said Jamie Dimon of JPMorgan. "Wherever you go, you're on. There's always a great team with me on trips but the CEO himself or herself often has to do the five town halls, the interviews, the client meetings. You can have all the senior help in the world but often you're the one who's front and center."

I heard that a lot. The sheer physical nature of the job was daunting. Teresa Taylor, the former COO of Qwest, described it like this: "I didn't realize how programmed my schedule was, because, you know, you have things scheduled out a year in advance. And it's just every day, my assistant would hand me my schedule, and it's run, run, run, run. And I didn't have a lot of choices because there were a lot of obligations. When I left [the office], I thought, you mean, *I* can decide if I want to do this? And the great part about leaving was I could have lunch with who I wanted to, not with who I *had* to."

Ask the Boss: How Do You Hire?

Maybe CEOs can't tell us what to do next but they can surely tell us how they view their staff and what they think of them.

For instance, *what do they look for when they hire?*

"I look for probably taking the time to get a good education," Martin Sorrell, the CEO of WPP, one of the world's largest advertising agencies, said. He employs over 170,000 people. "Obviously, some people don't have the wherewithal or the family support or the family means to get a good education, but I'm a big believer in a good undergraduate and postgraduate education. I'm a big believer in business schools. I've often said other things being equal, if there were two candidates, I'd choose the business school graduate over the nonbusiness school graduate, which is a view that many people do not share and think is crazy. But I think if somebody has made the effort to go to business school and think about business and do that for the two years or so that you spend at a good school . . . the fact that these schools are self-selecting, the chances are that the people that come out of them are going to be better than those who don't."

A good many of them spoke about the importance of consistency. Nobody wanted to see a potential candidate jump around a lot from job to job. Outside of Silicon Valley, where high growth means high turnover, it was hard to find any CEO who thought brief stints at companies was good for one's career.

"I think you can't ignore first and foremost, the record of the people," said Ralph Schlosstein at Evercore. "How have they done in school? And this is entry level hiring I'm talking about. The breadth of their interests. I can normally tell within five minutes of meeting someone, whether it's someone who I would want to hire or not, just from whether there is a sparkle in their eyes and a curiosity and interest about them.

"The one thing I don't like is people who have four or five firms on their resume. Whenever we hire someone, my expectation is that they'd spend the rest of their career at the firm. But if somebody has been in five different places already and you hire them, chances are after two or three years, they're going to go to a seventh place."

I think there are a few exceptions to this view. One is that when you're young, you jump around a lot. I know I did. When I graduated college, my first job lasted four months. The second lasted two years. And then I kept moving position after position every two to three years. I was too afraid to buy a home anywhere because, I thought, in a few years I'd leave. But to Ralph's point, after a while your career matures and you find a place you clearly want to make your career in.

Other reasons you might jump around are that you've switched careers and are starting all over again or you've been laid off and needed to find your footing, even if that meant taking a job that you didn't exactly want. But those jumps can be easily explained in an interview.

Elon Musk said there are only two questions he asks every candidate.

"One is to just explain the path of their careers," he said. "Why they made those decisions that lead from one role to the next. And the second one is to list evidence of exceptional ability. And academics is just one element."

Among the other elements he looks for: winning competitions.

"It's probably more important than academics. So if somebody has won the Formula SAE which is where you have to design and build a racecar and then race it and win, if somebody has really done well at that, that's much more valuable than getting a 4.0 GPA and way harder."

Later I found out Elon was talking about the head of the structures team at Tesla, who had won the Formula SAE and whose grades were nowhere near straight *A*'s.

When asked the question on what he looks for in a candidate, Jamie Dimon said it's not about the resume, but the story.

"I often say there's a book on everybody," he said. "There's a book on you right now. I don't really know the book on you but if I wanted to know I don't need to talk to you at all. I can talk to your friends, bosses, peers, subordinates, ex-partners, or boyfriends and I would know. I would know how hard you work, whether you show up on time, if you're trustworthy, whether you keep your word, whether you're a great friend, I'd know all of that. And we write our own books. It's really amazing—you almost don't have to meet the person."

Jamie went further and said if you talk to enough people, you start to get a feel for the entire company.

"One of the first things I did when I got here, I take everyone around [for breakfast, lunch, dinner]. I'd get to know people . . . and I'd ask what do you read? Who do you talk to? What's going on? Who do you trust in the company? And after a little time or maybe a little martini, you'd be shocked how consistent it is regarding who people trust and who they don't."

"The same names come up?" I ask.

"The same names and the same themes," he replied.

Jim Reynolds had an interesting take, one that matched the high growth nature of his company.

"The first thing I look for is bandwidth. Can that person process where we want to go? Not where we are today. I know this organization is changing and I am looking to buy companies and do different things. Do they have the bandwidth to go with me?

"One of the other things that's important to me is how much of a team player they are. Is the individual just about them and do they really want the career to be about them or are they somebody that looks at a goal and says, 'We got that done, we did,' or will they say, 'I did it, I led the team?'"

"How can you tell that in an interview?" I asked. "Everyone is going to say they're a team player."

"It goes back to listening. When you hear people say, 'I made this happen' or 'I did this' and if you drill down and listen if they say 'me' versus 'my team and I.' Again, it goes back to those leading questions. I'll ask, 'When you were on the trading desk, how did you work together?' and if they say, 'No, I took my own capital and I did this . . .' or if you ask, 'What kind of research did you do?' and they said, 'I did all my own research, our department was useless with research.' You just listen to the answers."

Every CEO admitted he or she has made hiring mistakes. No formula is foolproof.

"I think the biggest mistake that I made earlier when I was younger, just from starting companies, was to put too much emphasis on an individual's ability as opposed to their personality or how they affect others around them," Elon said. "I mean, it was really quite dumb because you should always evaluate somebody's contribution to the company net of how they affect others. At the very beginning of PayPal, when it was called X.com, I had one really smart individual but he was just not a good guy. He was really manipulative . . . it kind of really weakened the beginning of the company. And I actually made the mistake again at the beginning of Tesla. So you've got to take somebody's ability and then also ask, are they a good person? That's actually pretty important."

Ralph Schlosstein said at his firm, they have the "no jerks rule."

"Sometimes we might say no assholes in less polite company [*laughing*]. [My partners and I] all feel pretty passionately about that. I remember two people who we interviewed last year. Roger Altman and I both interviewed them. They were inarguably talented and inarguably would have produced a lot of revenue for the firm. After we both met with them, we said we really have to recruit them aggressively. And we checked them out at the two places that they had been before and both of them came back as profoundly 'I' people rather than 'we' people. And we just stopped the discussions."

"These people were clearly talented," I said.

"Yeah, they were extremely talented, but not at the expense of the culture and the teamwork within our firm. And you know, notwithstanding the fact that most people in our business have a pretty high opinion of themselves, some of the people I interview are legends in their own minds [*laughter*]. But investment banking really is a team sport and there are very few situations where one person knows everything."

In my own way, I could relate to that pressure of always being on. There are no bad days allowed on television. You can't walk onto the studio set and let on that your nanny just quit and you're having a bad hair day. You have to be in the moment and focused on the task at hand. But at a certain point, I can turn it off. When the lights go down, I can go back to being a "normal" person. CEOs can't. Everywhere they go, they represent their company. Any look, comment, smile is interpreted and misinterpreted a thousand different ways by their staff. Add on the pressures of a moving stock price and it's easy to see why being a CEO requires a kind of athleticism.

Chris Burch, the CEO of C. Wonder, who helped his ex-wife Tory Burch create their fashion empire, said wherever he goes, people are pitching him an idea.

"I don't mind it. It's kind of part of my job," he said. "It can get a little overwhelming."

"How often?" I ask.

"Like twenty people a day. They somehow know me and they pitch me. But I like the fact that I'm open. I actually love people and I want them to be successful. I really care about them."

"I always thought CEOs sat by themselves and made big powerful decisions," said Tim Armstrong, the CEO of AOL who was in the throes of restructuring the company. "The thing most people don't realize, at a small or big company, the CEO's job at the end of the day is a team job where you play on a team. That is probably the most surprising thing for me. The unpleasant part of the job is there are some decisions that only *you* can make. And some decisions are not pleasant. There's times when you have to put the organization ahead of your own personal feelings."

"A friend of mine just became the CEO of a big company," Jamie Dimon continued. "I said there are two things you're going to really notice. Number one is you can't complain to anyone anymore about how things work because it's you at the top . . . and the second is that even if you don't think you're making decisions when someone is presenting to you, just by listening and nodding you are giving tacit approval. Someone may come into your office and ask about *A, B, C,* and *D* and I'll be nodding. That person goes out believing that it's been approved. The CEO has a veto."

I asked him to explain further.

"It means you may walk into my office and say, 'I'm going to buy this and sell that, investigate this, negotiate that, and pay this amount.' I don't have to say a word but the fact that I didn't veto it says you have approval.

"*You* are now the person giving that approval or making the decision and there's no one else there with that role," he added, turning around and waving at the empty air behind him. "For a lot of these big companies, there are no real road maps. So you can look at what happened before, you can look at how someone else did it. It's not necessarily a road map for what you're dealing with, though it might be. Sometimes there are clear road maps but often there are not and you have to deal with it as you see it."

Which led to another revelation as I continued interviewing CEOs: the job is quite lonely.

"I have a great team at Cisco, really good people, but when it really gets tough as a leader, you are by yourself. It is lonely and that is something you just have to realize," John Chambers, the CEO of Cisco, said. "Now that doesn't mean you don't reach out to the team. It doesn't mean you don't listen to the team or your board of directors, but the leader has to know when the pressure's really on. It is one of the loneliest jobs in the world. You ask any CEO who's really been in the firing line . . . you might need to say, 'Is leadership really lonely especially when you're under pressure?' and you can watch their pupils dilate if you hit the person who's been through that. It is *really* lonely."

One research and consulting firm already asked a group of CEOs, half of whom agreed with John. According to a 2012 study by RHR International, 50 percent of the CEOs they surveyed who ran businesses topping out at $2 billion in revenue said they experienced loneliness in their jobs. Sixty-one percent believed the isolation hindered their performance. It was worse for freshman CEOs.

This is apparently not a new revelation. David Nadler, the vice chairman of Marsh and McLennan and an advisor to many CEOs in his long career, described the loneliness issue in a 1998 book, *Executive Teams*.

"Through the mid-1980s, a CEO could easily serve out a normal tenure without ever experiencing a true period of discontinuous change," he wrote in a chapter aptly titled "The World of the CEO." "From the mid-1980s to the early 1990s, with the restructuring of U.S. business and the growing intensity of foreign competition, there was a high probability that a CEO would encounter one cycle in which he would have to manage discontinuous change . . . the toll this responsibility takes on CEOs, on a very personal level, should not be underestimated."

And as if to further underline the isolation, Nadler drew this chart of the CEO, which he permitted me to use. The first thing I thought of was "the eye of the storm."

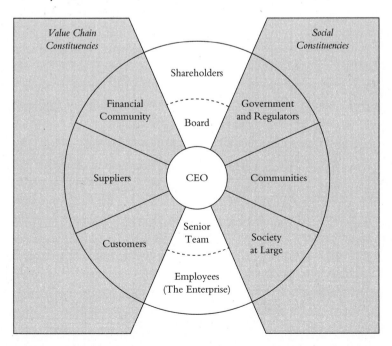

Over a decade later, pressures have only exponentially grown for the office of the CEO—from foreign competition, to stock price volatility, to shareholder activists. At the time of this writing, retailer J.C. Penney had just ousted its CEO, Ron Johnson, for getting rid of the heavy discounting shoppers loved. He'd been on the job for 17 months. Bill Lynch was also booted after just three years on the job leading Barnes and Noble. His strategy of focusing on the e-book side of the business wasn't gaining any traction. People, including Nolan Bushnell, were calling time on Tim Cook's leadership at Apple, saying he had only 12 to 18 months to prove he could keep creating *Jobs-esque* products.

And when you think about it, the financial crisis of 2008 was a great equalizer when it came to snuffing out who was the best bank CEO and who was the worst. Who fell down during the crisis and who rose to the occasion? Very quickly, CEOs like Merrill Lynch's Stan O'Neal, Citigroup's Chuck Prince, Lehman Brothers' Dick Fuld—guys who had been doing just fine so long as everything was running well—got cut down. You've never heard from them again. It's as if they vaporized into thin air, albeit with their millions in the bank.

But others, like John Mack at Morgan Stanley, Lloyd Blankfein at Goldman Sachs, and Jamie Dimon at JPMorgan saw the pending storm and bolted down the hatches. They ran their firms against the wind and ate up the smaller guys. Some became villains like Blankfein, whose firm was famously described as a "giant vampire squid" by *Rolling Stone* writer Matthew Taibbi. But you can't deny that Blankfein confidently led Goldman through the crisis and has emerged atop the heap, a little weathered with a beard, but still on top. Jamie Dimon came out of the financial chaos looking like General George Patton, the man who could not be shaken. Although by the time I met with him, he was facing another, more personal challenge. Angry shareholders were threatening to vote him out of the chairman's role over the trading scandal in London.

"To me, the financial crisis separated the good and the bad CEO," said Jim Reynolds. "It makes you think about the power of that seat. The good ones are the true visionaries because when you sit in that seat, the buck stops with you. By the time it gets to your desk, you cannot point the finger at anyone else. That is the only seat in the firm that's like that. You have to have the vision, focus, discipline, passion, intelligence, a strong sense of self, and confidence. But not hubris, because that can lead you in the wrong direction. The ability to make decisions based on good information and then when you're wrong, change those decisions *immediately*."

"I think I would want to ask other CEOs, 'Who are the two, three, four people they surround themselves with to ensure they can be successful?'" said Susan Lyne, the former CEO of the luxury retailer The Gilt Groupe and now head of AOL Brands. "Most CEOs can't do that job without a really great inner circle and that doesn't mean your direct reports. I would love to hear how different people put together the office of the CEO."

"I ask other CEOs: How do you run your place? I call them and ask, 'What do you do? How do you actually run it?'" Jamie said. "And you'd be surprised for some people there are no formal meetings— Warren Buffett for example. For others, they get on the road and out in the market often. One way is not necessarily better than the other but I always ask successful leaders: How do you do it?"

"Have you modeled yourself on anybody?" I ask.

"No, but I've learned from watching all of them. Bob Lipp [the former JPMorgan board member] I used to work with, he just had a great way with people. Bob used to have the Hall of Shame. He'd put the stupidest memo up on the wall. I was up there once or twice. But he made it fun for people. It was his way of killing bureaucracy. I remember Bob at the end of the year would call the top 50 branches and just congratulate them, ask them what did you do so well? And I took note about sharing best practices like that."

"I have not been a CEO, but I ran our investment bank for almost two decades and I have spent most of my career advising CEOs," Jimmy Lee, who sits a few doors down from Jamie at JPMorgan, said. "And I agree it can be lonely at the top. It's also windy at the top. That's why you need to build that great team around you and make sure that team is doing the same thing with their people. The French have an expression: *The graveyards are full of indispensable men . . . and women.*"

The discussion about loneliness and isolation made the office a little more human. For a majority of us, we have bosses we have to defer to, people who make final decisions, and who, in many ways, determine our future career paths. But we also have colleagues to socialize with and mentors to seek advice from. CEOs are the be-all and end-all in their organizations. They make the final decisions. They're at a table for one. I imagine it can be a scary place because you don't have many people you can bounce ideas off of.

Ask the Boss: What Does Open-Door Policy Really Mean?

Most CEOs say they have an open-door policy but do they really?

"I think our culture starts with the fact that the door to my office has never been closed and I've been in this office now for twenty years," said Sam Zell. "This is a conscious choice that tells people in more than words that everyone has access to me. Anyone can come in anytime to talk about issues, deals, whatever. About ten years ago, I put M&Ms in a bowl on a table in my office when somebody sent me a bunch of them. Today, people walk into my office, take some M&Ms, and leave, and often don't even say hello!

"What I'm really talking about is access. The fact that I interface with everybody, that I see everybody walking past the door and people say hi, that means you're involved. In so many corporations, the contact levels are very rigid and people don't go much beyond their own levels to inter-act. If you're the CEO, you have five direct reports. Those are the only people you talk to regularly, your only source of information."

The reality is that many of us *do* work in hierarchical com-panies. But that doesn't mean the CEO is not accessible. I spent many years at several companies never thinking once I could simply call up the CEO's office and request a meeting. But apparently, this happens.

"I have to tell you, I was just always amazed that gener-ally the very young talent in the company had no problem calling my office directly and demanding to have time with me," Teresa Taylor said. "And I always took it because I was always intrigued by this—just to have the *guts* to do that. If they have the guts to pick up the phone, talk to my secretary and say, 'I need time with her, I'm a first-level manager in this company and I deserve it,' which is generally their attitude, I'd say, 'Bring them in.'"

I wondered what came out of these meetings.

"I'm sure it didn't go the way they wanted, because it usually started with, 'What is this company going to do for me, to manage my career?' Those were the words—'me' 'my'—and I would usually say, 'Nothing. What are you going to do for yourself?' And the conversation always went a different direction. I would say probably fifty percent of the people walked out saying, 'That was awful. Oh, my God, what was I thinking?' The other fifty percent said, you know, 'Thanks, and I appreciate it.' And I would hear from those people later in life."

It was good advice from Teresa. If you're going to spend 15 minutes with the CEO of your company, better to show him or her what you can do for them rather than pry out of them what they think of you. I thought of what Susan Lyne said about gravitating towards people who can give her feedback, people who do not necessarily report directly to her.

It's a delicate line to maneuver. Once you're in the meeting, the CEO is wondering why you're there. Harvey Golub said of his time at American Express, "Anybody could get to me, but for somebody who didn't report to me, if they called and said, 'I want to set up a meeting with Harvey,' my secretary would have asked 'What about?' She probably would have set it up and if a person came in to complain about his boss, I would say, 'Well, let's get your boss in here. Let him hear what you're saying as well.' So you do those things carefully. You don't abuse the privilege of being the boss."

Harvey is a friendly but measured person. From the brief times I've met and had lunch with him, he's very thoughtful, opinionated, and blunt. I can imagine some personalities mesh well with his and others don't. But that's just a fact of personal relations. Some people you can easily talk to and others you can't. And some CEOs you can easily sit in an office with and chat away and others, well, you might be checking the clock after 10 minutes.

And very few CEOs take it to the accessibility level like Jamie Dimon or Warren Buffett. Warren, as I mentioned, is in the rarefied group of rock-star CEOs. Investors travel from all over the world to meet him in Omaha. Athletes, celebrities, billionaires come to see Buffett to glean his advice. At the Berkshire annual meeting one year, U2's front man, Bono, strolled under the dome of the CenturyLink stadium to hear Buffett speak.

And every year, planeloads of students visit. It's almost as if Warren Buffett is his own foreign exchange student program.

"Students ask me that all the time, how do I find [what I love to do]?" Buffett said. "I just tell them you keep looking and you'll know it when you see it. I can't promise you that it will be tomorrow, or next week, or next year." He mentioned in a few months he would be hosting another group of students from the Middle East.

Jamie Dimon, in the meantime, hosts employees on the JPMorgan bus he rides across the country, visiting clients and branches. He opens up his collar, trashes the tie, and dons the cowboy boots in say, Austin, Texas, where he was in February 2013.

"I say to people that when they come on the bus they have immunity. We do it in groups and it is fun for people. I often start off by saying 'So there's a reason you're all here. Tell me where we can be better or where we're messing up.' I tell them about some stupid practices another group told me about. And they're all laughing because they've been frustrated by the same thing."

"Do you hear from them afterwards?" I ask.

"Sure, I get e-mails and other comments. We track their ideas. We follow up on every idea so they know we weren't kidding."

I asked if there was an example of an idea that was followed up on.

"Hundreds. There are hundreds. We've learned that tellers should be more involved in the design of the teller systems because they're the ones that have to use it. One teller told me that she and her colleagues would have to go through an entire account opening process with a new customer only to find out afterwards through another process that the customer was not eligible for that service. In hindsight it seems obvious we should have switched the order of how we were bringing these customers on board. And since then, we've saved thousands of wasted hours. There are hundreds of these types of examples that still pop up."

A few months later, Jamie Dimon handily won the vote to keep his chairman's title. He won it by a bigger majority than expected. Headlines blared that now the "Cult of Jamie" had been cemented. One financial blogger asked, "Is Jamie Too Big to Fire?" All of those news stories inevitably raised the other question: What happens if Jamie gets hit by the bus? Who will take his place?

For a CEO, the questions are never ending.

"Once you become CEO, you suddenly realize you're generally not getting tacit approval for your decisions," Jamie said. "You have the company board but they're not making the day-to-day decisions." I recalled how Warren Buffett said if his board started meddling in his work he'd tell them to stick it up their backsides.

Another CEO mused that if he started asking his senior managers for advice because he was unsure of a decision, he'd set off a panic. "They look to *you* to know what you're doing. If you tell them you have no idea if something is going to work, suddenly they get worried and wonder if you can lead and where the company is headed," he said.

And even if CEOs were to ask for input from the people under them, it's not guaranteed they would ever get the true answer. Ralph Schlosstein, the CEO of Wall Street firm Evercore, said that was the first thing he noticed after getting the corner office.

"I would say that probably the biggest thing that I gained an appreciation for, which I just didn't have an appreciation for before, is how hard you have to work to make sure that people really give you their honest opinion," he said. "The deferral to seniority is such a natural instinct. You get to know that there are some people who are never going to tell you the truth. And it's not that they are constantly lying to you. They just feel that it jeopardizes their career to express a view different from yours."

I asked him what someone should do if they wanted to express a different opinion.

"I'd say number one, think really carefully about how you're going to phrase it. Think through all aspects of it. And I would say those types of things are often best done in one-on-one private conversations."

Teresa Taylor, the former COO of Qwest, felt the same way as Ralph.

"Everybody filters the information for you," she said. "Everybody wants to tell you everything is going to be okay, when it's not. It's all orchestrated. So it's really hard to get to the truth."

She said she would get out of her office and "walk the floors" to see what was really going on at the company.

"I'd even just stand in the back of the room and I would just chat with someone and after a while they would say, 'You look familiar,' and I'd say, 'Oh yeah, I work here,' and I would just try to keep it real low key because that's when people would open up. So it's a lonely job, no question about that."

Granted there are the major perks—the huge pay packages, the amenities like a corporate jet, the glamour of being invited to all the glittering events. "There's definitely an ego trip to people waiting for you to walk in the room, people asking you, do I want a Diet Coke and they already knew I liked Diet Coke. All those little things are a total ego trip, you know?" Teresa said.

Diet Coke: The Choice of a CEO Generation

If there was one consistent theme throughout my interviews with CEOs, it was that they all seemed to drink the same thing during the day.

Diet Coke.

I already knew Warren Buffett drank Coke. Specifically, Cherry Coke (he also sat on the board of Coca-Cola for 17 years and is its biggest individual shareholder).

But other CEOs mentioned Diet Coke. Elon Musk has it stocked in his refrigerator. Maybe Diet Coke is the new black coffee.

John Chambers put a spin on the Diet Coke: He used it as cover to get a break.

"Every meeting I have, there's not even five minutes between them, sometimes not even 30 seconds," he said. "So what I originally did was I walked over and got a Diet Coke and walked back. That would allow me time to frame my question for the next meeting, finish up my prior meeting before I go in."

That worked very well, he said, until "people started bringing my Diet Cokes to me."

No ego trip was enough, though, to attract anyone to the job of CEO of AIG. AIG was probably the most hated company during the 2008 financial crisis, when its financial products division essentially blew up the financial system and cost Americans millions of jobs. By the time Bob Benmosche, who had retired from MetLife years ago and was growing grapes in his Croatian vineyard, got the phone call, the government had run out of options. Nobody wanted the job. I imagined it like the Gotham Police calling Batman—someone dark and mysterious had to save the world. Except in this case Batman was a silver-haired insurance executive.

"I was done. I said at sixty-two years old . . . I wanted to focus on my personal life," Bob recalled. "My wife and I have been separated for a long time and I had another relationship which was important to me and I wanted to just figure out what life is all about. Once, I said to [former AIG CEO] Hank Greenberg, 'We did research at MetLife and I'm going to tell you the outcome, but it's a secret. And after years of study we found out that everyone dies. And not only did we find that out, but we found out also that they don't get to take it with them.' And so you have to say to yourself, 'When is enough enough?' And find other things to enjoy and so I chose to focus on my home in Dubrovnik . . . it took six years to do this project.

"I started my vineyards in 2006, two of them. And I decided to become a winemaker. And so I started planting grapes and going up and seeing how the grapes were growing," he continued. "It was a little boring. I was retired for three years and life was good."

After the AIG board and government officials convinced Bob to take on the job to turn around AIG, "I told everybody I'm going to be vicious and aggressive. I'm going to complain about everything that's been done and then I'm going to fix it. But you need to understand when I'm asked I'm going to tell them that I think [people in Congress] are nuts."

Bob's exact words the first time he met with AIG employees was that he thought Congress was filled with a bunch of "crazies" and they could "stick it where the sun don't shine" if the lawmakers called him out to Washington to testify. Those quotes howled through the halls of Congress and turned Bob into both a troublemaker and a hero.

"It became clear that there isn't anybody in Washington that wants me within 100 miles of the place. But that's why even Elijah Cummings [Democratic congressman from Maryland] surprised me when he went on TV after some of those comments and he said, 'Look, he's got a good reputation. We're going to give him the benefit of the doubt. He just shouldn't bite the hand that's been feeding him. But for now I have nothing further to say but let's see how he does.' And that's the last I heard from anybody in Congress. So part of the whole intent was the people in this company had to understand that I have an f— you attitude and that I'm going to do it. Here's what I'm going to do."

Bob's ordeal reminded me of what Jamie would go through three years later in 2012 with the $6 billion London Whale trading fiasco, when a few rogue traders threatened to take down the entire firm.

Or what Warren Buffett went through in the 1980s, turning around Salomon Brothers after trading fraud sent Congress on a witch hunt. There are, as Jamie said for a CEO, no road maps.

"I wanted to explain to people that you need to get past your fears right this minute—not next week, not next month, but right *now*. And I will *represent* you," Bob said, leaning in. "I had one person, several of their kids were beat up. One man said to me, tears in his eyes, I just felt badly for him because he couldn't control it, he said, 'Bob, my third-grade daughter was asked to stand in front of the class and the teacher said, 'This young lady's father is an executive with AIG and they destroyed the whole financial system and isn't that sad what her father did.' And he said, 'Bob, what am I going to do?'. . . One of our employees in financial products wrote me a note thanking me for his career and everything else and he wrote, I've got it here," Bob said, pulling up his BlackBerry. "'The work you have performed here has been absolutely amazing and for me it started with your first trip to Wilton,' which would have been August 10. The first day I'm working I went to Wilton, Connecticut to speak to the folks there whom at the time was the center of blame for what it seems was everything that was wrong with America. But that's just one person, one example of many e-mails I get."

"Do people just e-mail you freely like that?" I asked.

"Yeah, I get lots of e-mails."

"Do you try to answer all of them?"

"I answer every one of them."

"You do?"

"Immediately . . . except if I'm in a meeting for three or four hours. I go through my e-mails pretty quickly because I think that's the most important thing . . . getting a response from me is a big deal. I get that it's because it's the CEO of AIG. Getting a response right away from me versus the secretary is a big deal.

"In the old days I used to get mail sent to me, I would handwrite a note on it. I don't do that anymore because I just don't have time. I made sure I wrote a note, I signed it, 'Bob, thanks for the input,' whatever. And they would have it on their desk. They would say, 'Bob just sent this . . . you think he doesn't read this shit? Man, look at that, he wrote it with his own handwriting.' No form letter, no secretary, it's my handwriting that says that son of a bitch had to sit down and write that. And some days it gets hard but it spreads the word that I'm accessible, so don't screw around because he's everywhere and you don't know *where* I'm going to be and *when* I'm going to be there. And that's part of keeping an organization on its toes."

When I asked Bob what it's like to be a CEO, he thought about it for a while and replied, "You know the Sword of Damocles?"

I shook my head no. Bob went on to recount the ancient Greek tale of the courtier named Damocles who envied his king.

"He said to the king, 'Oh, you have the best life and it's great, and look at all the lavish parties and the riches you have.' And the king said, 'Well, if you want to know, have a life like mine, I'll show you what it's like.' And so what he did was, he had him sitting at the table feasting with them, and then he looked above him and he saw this giant sword above his head and it was hanging by a thread. And he realized that the thread could snap at any second and he would die. And he was very uncomfortable about sitting underneath that sword, but he got the picture. And so when you're a CEO the problem is you have that sword hanging over your head at all times. And you can make the mistake of thinking that you've made it, but it's not a good thought to have. You've got to figure out a way to keep moving and keep leading and recognizing that everybody in this company now looks to you for their leadership and you have to be responsible for their lives. You can come in and the place is in good shape, a lot of people around. You go to your office and enjoy the trappings and the fancy lunches and dinners and the planes and so on. But sooner or later you've got to run the company. And sooner or later when something goes wrong in the night, you've got to figure out how to fix things."

★★★★★★★★

Anne Mulcahy, the former CEO of Xerox, joked that private equity is the place where CEOs go to die.

"I said that's the one thing I won't do," she said. "That's like a near-death experience going into private equity for a retired CEO."

She raised an interesting point. What happens after you've been king or queen of your domain?

Ask the Boss: What Holds People Back?

With all this talk about what CEOs look for when they hire, I began asking them about *what holds people back in their careers?*

Chris Burch, the retailing CEO, at first said fear. But then as he talked, he revealed a secondary issue that I could relate to as well.

"I think the number one mistake [people] make is they're concerned about their careers, how they're perceived, and I think they should be concerned about, ultimately, do they make their boss' life better?" he said. "Do they make their customer's life better? And do they make the company better? And I think those people always move to the top. And they also are willing to say it straight."

It made me think back to what I learned about likability and the four magical words one can ask someone else, "How can I help?" Perhaps that phrase is not said enough and I admit that, at more times than I'd like to mention, I've been remiss in that area. Aim to go into your meetings, lunches, and conversations with the idea of how you can help and you'd be surprised at the responses after a while. Oftentimes your help is not needed but you become the person who is seen as helpful to the organization, rather than the problem child. I'm reminded of what Bruce Ratner told me, how sometimes he keeps average employees simply because they're the "glue" people. They keep the morale up and the organization together.

"I think the biggest thing that holds people back is they don't tell people what they need or want—what I call 'Ta-Da' moments," said Tim Armstrong, the CEO of AOL. "They do everything in the background and show up with work done and 'Ta-Da!' They don't take into account most people want to help. Before there were organizational charts, before PowerPoints, in the beginning of the industrial age, there were no review processes. It was business on the fly—you had to give constant feedback, there was a fluidity between managers and employees. Nowadays, people build up their whole thing to communicating once a year versus having an ongoing eco-system. I think that holds people back."

It was an interesting concept, as I myself have committed this crime, and I have seen plenty of others, men and women, do the same thing. Part of that is a fear of raising any issues with superiors. "If I quietly do my work, then my boss will appreciate when it's all done," the thinking goes. While your intentions may mean well, you may come across as controlling or secretive or *not* a team player. Another issue is what Sam Zell and Martin Sorrell both described as a disease among the stars of an organization: They want to keep all the information to themselves until they can reveal it without someone stealing their ideas or to use it for bartering purposes. That got one woman fired by Sam, and Martin has had to constantly manage the hoarding tendencies in his own company.

"I think the biggest mistake people make is they don't have their own rudder," Teresa Taylor said. "They don't have their own ethics and their own morals clear. That's usually what gets anyone in trouble . . . it's like their heads get too big, their ethics get out of whack, and then pretty soon, before you know it, they're kind of bending the rules, they're bending the expense accounts . . . all these things sort of start happening."

Many of us are happy to retire into a quiet life, have the freedom to travel or pursue our hobbies and spend time with our families. But CEOs, leaders, driven type-A personalities are a little different—instead of going from zero to 60 everyday, they're suddenly on the bus again when they leave the top job. Much was made when Mitt Romney, the Republican presidential candidate, saw his security detail disappear overnight once he lost the election to President

Barack Obama. Using the codenames "Javelin" for Mitt and "Jockey" for Ann Romney, on the morning after the Tuesday vote, the Secret Service radioed out, "Javelin, Jockey details, all posts, discontinue." Days later, a photo emerged on the Internet of Romney pumping his own gas.

Al Gore famously got fat and grew a beard after he slipped into the post-election blues. Others become the opposite, like Jimmy Carter, whose disastrous presidency energized him to prove to the world he was fit to be president, even though he was voted out of the White House after one term.

When I ask some CEOs about life after the office, one didn't even want to contemplate it. Another mentioned a welcome relief of being able to play golf and hang around with family and friends whenever he chose. Several did not rule out another job in the future, albeit at a smaller company or a startup. And almost all joined boards or became advisers to yes, private equity firms. Warren Buffett has joked they'd have to carry him out of the offices of Berkshire. He has no plans of ever retiring.

"My question [for other CEOs] would be more about life after," Anne said. "It's a very consuming role and no matter how hard you try to say that's not my life, it *is* our life. And I would love to talk to just some people who could provide some wisdom on the life after about how do you kind of translate all of that great stuff. And you literally go from being so important to not being important at all. I've got to tell you, it's one of the hardest things I've ever done and I'd love to talk to people who've done it well."

After leaving Xerox, Anne became chairman of the Save the Children fund. She has also been rumored from time to time for a Washington appointment.

As other people might put it, these are high-class problems to have. After all, a CEO usually won't have to worry about money for the rest of his or her life. They'll always circulate among the powerful and elite. But this question raises an important topic for the rest of us.

How do you create a purposeful life when one of the main purposes in your life is gone?

It's a difficult topic for anyone but even more difficult for people who have achieved great heights in their careers, leading to that common but true phrase: the higher you rise, the harder you can fall. Stories abound of movie stars who crash and burn into a world of drugs and addiction, or Olympic athletes who end up stocking shelves at the Walmart. Going back to the sports/CEO analogy, many former football and basketball players hit hard financial times after the games are over, spending the rest of their lives trying to recapture the glory of their twenties. Imagine if your career peaked in your twenties? What would you do to top that?

There are, of course, no clear answers. The fact is, a job can end at any time. It's up to you to always figure out *what's next?*

Sometimes the answer is you just always plan that you do something else. Here is where entrepreneurs and women have a leg up over other people. Entrepreneurs do so because it's in their DNA to always think about what else to do. They can't sit in one place for long. Nolan Bushnell, the Atari founder, declared with not the least bit of self-consciousness that the current company he is working on, BrainRush, will be his biggest success yet. Brainrush is an educational tool for students from kindergarten to twelfth grade that helps them sharpen their mental skills, the way chess playing does for Nolan. You can say it's a personal obsession of his, as he confessed his biggest fear is his brain turning to mush. "I want to be as sharp as Aunt Betty was at age 103."

"I believe that [BrainRush] will be explosive during the first half of 2014 and that I will sell the company in the fall of 2014 for a whole bunch of money," he said. "I have a really good sense of how things transpire and how you can market and get people to adopt. We have proven that we can teach kids ten times faster using this software. The results are so extraordinary. I know all the big players in the education field, I know what people think the obstacles are; we have ways to get rid of those obstacles. It sounds cocky, but I kind of get it."

Women have an advantage because, frankly speaking, the minute we enter the workforce, we have hanging over us the moment when we wonder what we do after children. I hit that moment in my late twenties. I never considered not working but the knowledge that at some point, I would take a three- to six-month break in my job made me think: Do I want to go back to my job? Do I want to try something new? Do I like what I'm doing and can I see myself doing it for the next twenty to thirty years? (For a brief moment, my sister and I dreamed we'd start a baby gifts company but that idea never made it off the paper.)

Ask the Boss: What's It Like to Fire People?

We may know people who've been fired but what's it really like to fire people?

Harvey Golub ran American Express for eight years and had to go through several restructurings.

"[Firings and layoffs] are really different," Harvey said. "Firing somebody is an individual action. So if you're firing somebody because they're incompetent, or they're unethical, or they stole, you're doing it because they're not quite up to the job. In some jobs you can tolerate some mediocre performance."

I asked him if he ever wanted to keep people he laid off because they were, unfortunately, employed in one division.

"Early in my tenure at American Express, we had to restructure parts of the operation, and one of the things we had to do is close an entire operating center. It was in Jacksonville, Florida, so there were 2,000 people laid off. Many of them were excellent people. What we did in that process was we, among other things, offered anybody there who had exceptional performance the right to bid on other jobs in other centers in Atlanta and Greensboro and South Florida and so on so that they could find other jobs. But there were excellent people in that operation."

"You had to lose them," I said.

"We had to lose them. We just closed the entire center. There was no choice. And those are terrible things, too. So you do them in the most humane way and you try and make the process as easy as possible and you try to do them in good times."

"So people can find another job?"

He nodded.

"Did you ever have guilt?"

"No, I didn't have guilt, because my responsibility was the entire company. Sometimes you do things like, do you cut off this limb or do you wait and let the whole tree die? You have to make those decisions because you don't want the tree to die. So you don't feel guilt. You feel sorry."

In 2012, 1.5 million people were involved in mass layoffs—the elimination of 50 jobs or more in a single event, according to the Bureau of Labor Statistics. Companies like Cisco, IBM, and Walmart have all had to let their people go in the last few years. In some cases, the circumstances were economics. In others, it was bad management. It didn't matter if it was a startup or an old, established corporation—companies all go through these cycles. Even young entrepreneurs eventually turn into "The Man" they grew up despising.

Like Ben Huh, the CEO of www.Cheezburger.com, a website that posts outrageous clips of animals. He laid off a third of his staff and told *Inc.* magazine about it.

> Twenty-four people were let go, bringing our head count to forty-two. It was the most difficult week I've ever experienced. Often, when faced with a problem, you want to run in the other direction. It's like seeing a lion in the jungle. But I have to do what is best for the company, even if it sucks emotionally.

Around the time I interviewed her, Sallie Krawcheck, one of the most prominent female executives on Wall Street, was contemplating the what's-next question. She'd already been fired in a public fashion from two big Wall Street firms but still managed to leave with her reputation intact. At Citigroup, she was ousted for a noble cause: advocating for the small investor. At Bank of America, she was turning a profit at the wealth management division but new management came in and cleared house.

Sallie told me how after her first firing, a senior woman executive said her career was over. I was shocked to hear that—it would have to take some balls (pardon my language) to tell someone that. I asked if she knew the woman well.

"No, no, it wasn't somebody I knew very well. It was a pretty prominent woman and what was fascinating is she didn't say it meanly. It was empathetically and sympathetically, as in 'I'm sorry that your career is over.' Now . . . look at the evidence. Name another woman in financial services who has been publically fired and then come back to another big role?"

"Not very many at all," I said, trying to think of any. There was Zoe Cruz, the former co-president of Morgan Stanley, who left and nobody heard about again. Erin Callan, the chief financial officer, of Lehman Brothers, who famously was put out on stage as a young, rising star during the financial crisis, only to be run over and thrown out when it was clear she had no idea what was really on the balance sheet of the firm.

"I can't think of any," Sallie replied. "So her comment comes from the history and the background."

"What did you say to her when she said that?"

"What are you going to do?" she said. "I thought, 'Well, that's a bummer. Oh, well. I'll show you.'"

She laughed again. "I'll show you."

Sallie was coy about what she'd do next. Wall Street was still in her blood but clearly she was hankering for a different direction. She alluded to meetings in Washington and on the West Coast. I didn't doubt she was a woman in demand—the reality is that prominent businesswomen are very scarce. There are only 20 women CEOs out of 500-listed Standard & Poor's companies and their public relations departments are unusually busy fielding requests to speak at almost every event.

A few months later, it was announced Sallie was buying the women's networking group, 85 Broads, from a former Goldman Sachs executive. Sallie was embracing her new role as a champion of women in the workplace.

In a *New York Magazine* piece, Sallie was quoted describing her career switch: "The women's issue kept popping up," she says. "I consider myself to be a recovering research analyst, and the numbers are just so damn compelling."

At the end of the piece, Sallie described exactly the issue that hits all CEOs when they leave, the issue that Anne Mulcahy was looking for wisdom and advice on, the topic that we will all confront, whether we love our jobs: *What do we do next?* Because, as Sallie described at the end of the magazine article, when she left Bank of America, Christmas cards delivered "were down by 95 percent."

Chapter 10

Sound Off: The Most Annoying . . .

I'm generally an easygoing person, but there are two things I find very annoying: People who drive way below the speed limit and people who wait until they get to the airport security officer before finding their ID.

Hey . . . we're all human! We have our pet peeves. I'd love to think nothing bothers the most enlightened of us but I imagine even the Dalai Lama gets irritated once in a while. CEOs are no different. So I asked them all what they found most annoying:

Martin Sorrell, CEO, WPP: "I hate voicemail when the voice says, 'I'm sorry, I can't get to the phone now.' I hate that. And I hate the e-mail back that says, 'I'm on a plane or I can't be reached' especially if it's urgent to speak to somebody . . . there was one case where, probably in our own organization, I sent [a person] an e-mail and he had on his e-mail response: 'I'm sorry, I'm away on holiday at the bottom of an olive grove. There is no Wi-Fi reception at the bottom of the olive grove.' And I went absolutely ballistic. I said, 'Get that thing off of there!' When you deal with a client and he gets that message, we'd probably be fired."

Warren Buffett, CEO, Berkshire Hathaway: "When [people] come up with eight one-dollar bills and ask me to sign them. As soon as I sign those, more people keep coming up!"

Sam Zell, CEO, Equity Group: "People invading my space."

Anne Mulcahy, former CEO, Xerox: "Having to tap into your Rolodex all the time. Being asked for favors all the time. How many people's kids can you get jobs for, people you haven't heard from in years all of a sudden appear . . . it's the never-ending set of requests."

Elon Musk, CEO, Tesla and SpaceX: "Being asked to speak at too many places. I actually don't like saying no. I don't like to turn people down . . . but it's literally impossible for me to run the companies and do [the speaking engagements]. I mean, seriously, I'm bored of hearing me."

Jamie Dimon, CEO, JPMorgan: "Game playing. Just tell me the truth."

Ralph Schlosstein, CEO, Evercore: "The most annoying thing is when there is a problem and it's not immediately communicated in the organization. When someone walks into my office and they say, 'We have a problem.' And I say, 'When did you first discover this?' They say, 'Ten days ago.'"

Sallie Krawcheck, CEO, 85 Broads: "I hate snarky tweets and anonymous rants. I hate that. I have this image of angry individuals sitting in the basement of their mothers' homes alone, in the dark, just popping off anonymously."

Tim Armstrong, CEO, AOL: "People build things up around the CEO position in their mind. . . . I don't like people creating pomp and circumstance around being a CEO. I want to get to know people personally."

Lou D'Ambrosio, former CEO, Sears Holding: "I'll give you three things that annoy me. One is when people tell me what they think I want to hear. I know what I think. Don't tell me what you think I want to hear. If I want to know what I thought, then I don't need your opinion. Number two, when it takes people a long time to get to the point. Get to the point up front. I get bored very easily. I have a lot of patience if the point is good. Then I want to hear the rest of it. And I would say the third thing is . . . when I send an e-mail to somebody, I do expect a relatively immediate response. Responsiveness is measured in hours, not days. And hours being, you know, single digits. And like low numbers."

Susan Lyne, CEO, AOL Brand Group/former CEO, Gilt Groupe: "The only time I get impatient is when someone who is working for me has not prepped for me something that's going to happen. I find myself at a meeting with no concept of what the end game is here. I have certainly had way too many experiences with people and thought, 'Oh my God, they've left me wide open.'"

Bob Benmosche, CEO, AIG: "I think the most annoying thing is people who are just overly arrogant. The 'Do you know who I am?' people."

Nolan Bushnell, founder, Atari, Chuck E. Cheese: "I really feel like people that are annoyed need to get over themselves. Give me a break. Go screw yourself."

Part Four

Things I've Learned

Chapter 11

You Can't Really Be Good at Everything . . . and That's OK!

R ecently on a shoot in Austin, I went back to my hotel room to rest up for the next morning. As usual, I woke up early. People have asked me how long I've been waking up at 4 A.M. to do my morning show. My usual reply is: "For so long that 6 A.M. is considered sleeping in."

The sad part is that's one hundred percent true. When I worked in newspapers, I would stay up all night writing my stories. I'm not sure why because my editors were all in London which meant the last deadline was usually around 6 P.M. East Coast time. There was no need for me to stay up all night filing a story that would not have been looked at until the next morning. Sometimes I think I wrote best when I knew my editors were asleep and not hounding me for the piece.

My night owl persona disappeared when I had my twins. No baby allows a mother to sleep until 10 A.M. I began watching lots of morning shows. I began to dream about being on one of those morning shows. Early morning hours felt like peace, before the babies began fussing and the day's work started. I came to understand why productive, type-A personalities liked to rise before dawn and head to the gym.

Which is all to say that on the morning in Austin, I woke up two hours earlier than I needed to—at 5 A.M.—and clicked onto a documentary on Bravo TV called *First Position*. It was about children who excelled in ballet, competing annually in New York for a rare spot at an elite ballet company. The storylines were all interesting, but the character that impacted me the most was a minor one. He was Jules Fogarty, the little brother of one of the more exceptional ballet dancers featured in the film, Miko Fogarty. For all his boyish charm, Jules was a personable but mediocre performer. Without the slightest bit of sympathy, the Russian teacher barked at him for not sucking in his belly. Jules stumbled around on stage. While his swan-like sister practiced late into the night, he was filmed snoring away on the mat.

To nobody's surprise except his mother, Jules quit ballet. He was a happier boy now, playing video games on his computer. When the documentary filmmakers interviewed his mother, she was sobbing away, expressing dismay for his decision to quit. "He said I don't have passion for ballet," his mother said in her Japanese accent. "I didn't imagine," she continued, wiping away her tears, ". . . when he quit I'm so sad."

At that point, I wanted to do that thing you're not supposed to do sitting in a hotel room by yourself, which was talk to the TV. I wanted to say "He's doing you a favor. He's not doing ballet because he's not very good at it and it only takes a 10-year-old to figure that out. And that's okay."

Bob Knight would understand what I'm talking about. Bob is one of the winningest coaches in college basketball history, known as much for his victories as for his temper. Whenever someone hears his name, they mention the "chair incident." You know the scene—the one where he threw a plastic chair across the basketball court after arguing over a foul call. He even made a commercial out of it for Volkswagen.

Bob must have been having a good day when he walked into our New York studio to talk about his new book, *The Power of Negative*

Thinking, because not only did I escape unscathed, but he agreed to chat after. The point that got him really fired up again was when I asked him about the parents of the players he recruits.

Every parent, he says, thinks their child is the next Kobe Bryant. The problem is not everyone is going to be good at everything and he wished parents would stop telling their children they could be whatever they wanted to be.

"I don't know how well society makes realistic statements to kids, sets up realistic opportunities to kids," he said. "It goes back to the 'whatever you want to be' thinking. Here's a classic example. When Mike Krzyzewski was at West Point, as a sophomore, I can't remember if I was first or second year as head coach, I said to him, 'We've got guys that can score better than you can, and can shoot better than you can. What I expect out of you is for you to handle the ball, make sure you're careful with it, hand it to the people who can score like Jimmy Oxley. You can't let Jimmy get in trouble.' Mike understood that and did a very good job for us. That was carried over to his coaching [*Mike later himself became one of the most famous coaches in college basketball, breaking Bobby Knight's record for wins*].

"A lot of people don't want to tell people they can't do this," he continued. "That lends itself to problems internally. But you're far better off telling people what they can't do to what they can do. Let them know that they're doing a good job."

Which doesn't mean you can't dream big. It only means that you dream where you have the biggest chance of success. And that's OK. Part of being an immensely successful person is to know what you're *not* good at. The problem is when someone believes he or she can do anything, when the talent clearly does not match up to the goal. Instead of a life of success, there is only disappointment and resentment.

Mario Gabelli is one of the most successful fund managers on Wall Street. He's worth hundreds of millions of dollars and still goes to work loving what he does. He's become rich in much the same way Warren Buffett has become uber-rich: by evaluating stocks and buying them for less than their intrinsic value.

Every success story has a beginning and Mario's began in the Bronx, where he was born. At the height of the 1970s recession, Mario Gabelli decided he wanted to start managing people's money so he decided to form his own firm.

"I made a decision in October of 1976 to start a broker–dealer. I didn't do the money management business because I didn't have the confidence yet I could raise money," Mario said. "But I knew I could make money for clients. On January 1, 1977, I started writing research, I was approved by the Securities and Exchange Commission, I had to lease space, get typewriters, letterheads, stationary. . . . I was able to get software, computer systems at a wholesale price."

Like any startup entrepreneur, Mario knew what he was good at and pursued it with a singular focus, even if it meant being his first and only employee. "At the time I was starting up, the telephone company was on strike, there were no payphones in our building so I was out on the street in a pay booth in the winter storm when one of my buddies passed by and said, 'Mario, when you said you were located on Wall Street, you really meant Wall *Street!*'"

Knowing what you're good at is actually a very difficult thing to do. It may sound easy but most people are in denial that they're bad at anything. Research shows, for instance, that most people think they're above-average drivers. You probably think you are, too.

Dan Portillo, the head of talent at the venture capital firm Greylock, sees this a lot. Entrepreneurs often have a hard time letting go control of the company they created. When I asked Dan how many of his entrepreneurs actually make good managers, he said, "My list of people that I think are phenomenal managers is pretty short." He went on to name four people out of the dozens of companies he manages in the Greylock portfolio. "Justin Fitzhugh who's now at Jive Software . . . he's a really great manager. I remember Justin was managing three teams that had nothing to do with each other but he just knew how to ask the right questions and get people focused around the right things. I think management is a skill that we don't really teach in Silicon Valley.

"The hardest point is when [the entrepreneurs] start to get that little bit of success for the first time and when you start dealing with growth, success, customers, and supporting those customers, that is when you figure out if someone is a good manager, too."

One of the smartest moves Mark Zuckerberg, the founder of Facebook, made was hiring Sheryl Sandberg. Where Zuckerberg was seen as the boy genius, she was the adult who knew how to run a growing company. Despite whispers at one point that Facebook may be the next Pets.com fiasco, the company is recovering from its disastrous initial public offering and growing like a steady, mature company with solid leadership.

Once you find the thing you're good at and you work tirelessly at it, that's when the possibilities open up.

Part of this goes back to something Warren Buffett said to me. He mentioned that students constantly ask him, "How do you find your passion? How do you know what you're good at?" As Buffett told his students, you just keep looking for it until you do. It's like looking for your soul mate—once you know it's right, it's right. It's in your gut.

Jamie Dimon could have become the home improvement king—but he listened to his gut and knew that was not his passion. Banking was in his blood. He described what happened after he was fired from Citigroup.

"The guys who ran Home Depot—Ken Langone and Bernie Marcus and Arthur Blank—called me up to discuss the CEO job before I went to Bank One. And I actually went down there and met with them and stayed at Arthur's house and went for lunch with them. I told them 'I have to confess that until you called me up, I had never been in a Home Depot.' They said, 'Oh we don't care, we like you as a person, the character, the integrity, the work ethic, we'll teach you.'

"They knew I wasn't going to *B.S.* them. But I would have been incapable of stepping into that job of CEO. I mean, I could not walk through a store and tell you whether it was a well-run store or not. I couldn't tell you whether the inventory was right, the merchandise was right."

"Did you walk through a Home Depot?" I asked.

"Yes, not just one but many with these guys."

"And you said, forget it?"

"No, no, I loved the whole thing. I loved everything about them, I loved the business. But the way I look at it, I needed to go back to what was really on my mind. Banking was the craft I'd been practicing for 20 years and I loved it. I understood trading floors and bank branches. I was confident I could run a financial company well. Moving outside of finance wouldn't have felt natural for me. It was more like if you play tennis your whole life and then you're told to go play golf."

★★★★★★★★

Back in Austin, I started to think more about why Jules resonated with me.

Maybe because I saw a little of myself in Jules.

When I was 12, my parents declared I would start to learn piano. My father had always threatened the possibility, but finally with the family more settled in Philadelphia and some time now on our hands, he found a music school for me to attend.

I could tell this was a real passion of his. He was very busy at the hospital, so for him to do actual research to find the best music school in the area and the best teacher meant he was serious. I remember being dragged on a rainy night (anything you don't want to do happens on a rainy weekday night) to the school, where my parents promptly registered me.

"You do want to play, don't you?" he asked me repeatedly and earnestly, to which I smiled meekly, "Of course! I do want to play." *Lies, lies, lies.*

My piano teacher was not nice. She was a fairly plump woman with Cher-like long hair and she did not smile kindly on me. My parents may have been clueless but she could tell right away I was not an admirer of her craft. She eyed my fingers and seemed to doubt right away they could stretch to the keys. She gave me what I thought were the most boring pieces of music to play, just to see if I would tough it out.

I dreaded each of those sessions but they went on for a year. When I heard she was leaving the school, I secretly smiled that this may be my excuse to stop the lessons. But instead, my parents asked that I continue the lessons at her house. God forbid, now I had to go to her dark, stuffy house.

And so I trudged over to her home for a few months more until finally, one day, either she couldn't take it anymore or I couldn't but she sat down exasperated and eyed me close.

"You don't really like playing, do you?"

"No, I really don't," I replied. "But my Mom and Dad think I can and want me to."

"Okay," she said, biting her lip. "You're . . . okay. You're not going to win any competitions. But if your parents are going to pay for these lessons, you may as well play something you like."

So together, for one reason or another, we picked the theme song to the sitcom, *Cheers*.

Unbeknownst to my parents, for a few months more, while they thought I was perfecting Johann Sebastian Bach's *Minuet in G Major*, I was opening the bar for Sam Malone and Diane Chambers. I memorized it all.

On Chinese New Year, my relatives all gathered at our house to celebrate.

"Si Si," my father called out to me, using my nickname. "Come play for your aunts and uncles what you learned."

You know how the story ends.

By the time I finished, there was dead silence. My relatives, many of whom had just arrived in the United States, thought it might have been a classical arrangement they missed because they were sheltered in China. My father made off as if he knew all along I was learning this.

But I heard nothing more. The lessons were cancelled and I never had to see Cher again.

The piano sits in his living room today, like a tombstone. It hasn't been tuned in years—actually, decades. I dare not play *Cheers* on it or else I might elicit a flashback. Although a few years ago, Dad did finally say to me, "I guess you never really liked it."

"No, I hated it."

But at least I knew what I was good at.

Chapter 12

Five Tips for Life

As you can well imagine, going around interviewing people about their careers eventually means the tables get turned on you. Several CEOs would, when there was a pause in the conversation, inevitably turn around and ask, "So what about you, Betty? What do *you* think?"

The truth is, it's difficult to sum up in a few short sentences. Some of what I'd heard from the interviews really resonated with me, particularly when Sallie Krawcheck and Susan Lyne described women holding themselves back or not speaking up when men had no problems doing so. Other topics made me feel I needed to work harder to improve myself, such as focusing more on what the other side needs in a negotiation. What I was glad to see was that nobody is perfect and in fact, many of the successful people have failed dramatically in their lives and been fired; some fired more than once. The fact that they were able to talk honestly about their failures only made me appreciate their confidence.

Jamie Dimon, for instance, recalled the day he got fired.

"I went home and I sat my three little girls down," he said. "They were probably at the time ten, eight, and six. I said, 'Girls, I've got to tell you something. I resigned, but that really means I no longer have my job. I was fired but I want you to know I'm completely okay.' And my little one said 'Daddy, do we have to go sleep on the streets?' I said 'No, sweetie, we're here, we're fine, we're fortunate everything's going to be exactly the same except Daddy's going to be home a bit more.' And the middle daughter who was always obsessed with college said, 'Can I still go to college?' I said, 'Of course you can still go to college.' And the oldest one said, 'So if everything's okay, can I have your cell phone? You won't be needing it.' Then one of the guys that works at the company came over, he was about six-foot-six. He knocked on the door and my little daughter answered, looking up and says 'Who do you want to see?' He says, 'I want to see your Dad. I work for your Dad.' She said, 'Not anymore you don't!'"

Sometimes I was surprised at how frank some of the CEOs were. John Chambers had no problem telling me he goes to the bathroom all day. There was a purpose to this, Chambers told me, and he learned it from a prominent lawyer during his days as a young executive at Wang Laboratories.

"He was getting very old, and he was retiring, and I said to him, 'Give me the lessons you learned that would be most useful to me.' He said, 'Whenever you have a chance to stop at the bathroom, I want you to stop,' and he laughed. He said, 'That will become more important as you get older.'

"He deliberately was quiet, because he was letting me think on it, and he said, 'Do you understand what I just told you?' I said, 'Yes, sir. I got it.' Whenever you finish a meeting, you want to finish that meeting, summarize what you're going to do and absolutely don't go to the next meeting still thinking about the prior meeting. Secondly, you need to develop techniques that allow you to reframe what you're going to get ready for in the next meeting, and you go in the next meeting knowing exactly what you want to accomplish. What are the two or three things you want to accomplish? Get your mind cleared of all distractions. You don't want any pressure on you. So the bathroom is a vehicle that reminds me of how to do that in my leadership style."

★★★★★★★★

Other CEOs were honest almost to an uncomfortable point—the discomfort being mine. Harvey Golub was very uninhibited in telling me that he thought the idea women were paid less than men was ridiculous.

"Any job [at American Express] that opened was public. You could bid on the job. Everybody got evaluated every year. We made sure the evaluations were clear and responsive. We told everybody what the performance of their unit in the company was and why," he said. "I remember getting a complaint once from a group of women who were saying that they were not being treated as well as comparable groups of men. They were senior professional executives. These weren't clerical people. They were lawyers and HR groups and so on. And we did a study and we found that actually they were treated better. They spent less time in a job before they got promoted. It took them a shorter period of time to get up to the median compensation in that position."

"Then why would they feel this way?" I asked.

"Because if somebody doesn't get promoted, the reason they're not being [promoted] is something other than themselves. The reason has to be in the stars."

He went on to note that on average, "but not true for any one individual, women tend to be a little more laid back, a little bit more relationship-oriented, a little less driven, more facilitative than men are.

"Years ago, forty years ago when I was with IBM, there was a question about whether women should become systems engineers because in those days women went to work in some career and then got married and left and raised children in larger numbers than would be true today. And so the question was, given that you're going to get higher turnover, should you put women in those jobs at all?

"I did an analysis and found the turnover was actually slightly less. It was just for different reasons. So women did leave because they got married and got pregnant in higher numbers than men, who never got pregnant and who never left for that reason. [Men] never left for getting married, but they left for different jobs . . . So the turnover rate for women was actually lower than for men. The causes were different."

"But there's a different perception," I replied.

"Exactly. It was the perception."

"Does it matter? A woman leaves a job for the family versus the man leaving for another job?"

"They're both leaving, so it doesn't matter in that respect," he said. "But the problem comes when you see phony statistics like the average woman earns less than a man . . . I mean, it is *so* not true. It's so not true but you hear that, and then you get equal pay for equal work. You get that kind of stuff and what you end up doing is reducing opportunities . . . it's been a while now but if you wanted to fire a minority or a woman, you went through a big, long process and everybody knew it. So you're better off putting a man in the job because you can fire him."

I could feel the ears of women executives around the country burning by those comments. But it was Harvey's perception and nobody can disallow someone's perception from being told, however right or wrong it may be. I went away from the lunch feeling that what Harvey described was spoken in the context of a career that began 50 years ago—much has changed since then.

Or had it? Sheryl Sandberg already stirred the pot with her book *Lean In*, arguing for exactly what Harvey said was a phony statistic: equal pay for equal work. Anne-Marie Slaughter, the senior policy official in the State Department who wrote the *Atlantic* article about how women could *not* have it all, touched off a firestorm. Her online article was one of the most read ever for the publication. Sallie Krawcheck was having her speak at a forum sponsored by 85 Broads. At the very least, people were talking about women in the workplace again and that had to be healthy.

One post on LinkedIn that caught my eye and that we featured on our television program was from a CEO in Belgium named Inge Geerdens. As head of a recruiting company, she articulated much of what I already personally felt in her blog post titled, "I'm Not Balancing Work and Life and I Feel Great."

"I don't need a balance," she wrote. "I'm not looking for a way to balance my private life with my professional life. I'm just trying to have a great life. Ever since I started my first company in 2003, my professional life has been taking up a lot of my time. There have been successes, failures, crises, expansions, new developments, and the challenges of day-to-day management. Sometimes a crisis forced me to skip a family vacation. Often I came home too late from work to tuck my children in. Does that mean my children are neglected? Of course not!"

Leave it to the Europeans to cut through our existential, middle-class American anguish.

What I Learned From My Kids

Susan Lyne said to me that she learns a lot from being a mother.

"I actually think the things you have to think about as a mother make you a better executive," she said. "There is no question that sensitivity to how something is going to play out with a person is something you learn as a Mom. How am I going to put this in a light that this person gets it? So that this three-year-old or four-year-old or thirteen-year-old gets it. Those are the kinds of issues we all face."

There are three things that I've learned from my kids.

1. *The simplest explanation is the best*. Most of the time when I ask them to explain something (and yes, this is usually when something wrong happens), they always surprise me with how simple their explanation is. "I don't eat the cheese you pack for me because it gets warm by the time lunch rolls around." "I kicked the cabinet door in and broke it because I was carrying a case of water. I'm sorry." There are no embellishments or big windup. They just explain and move on. I find I don't have much choice but to accept and move on too.

2. *Focus*. This was more relevant when they were younger and needed more of my attention. Nowadays, they would rather I leave the room while they play video games or hang out with their friends. As humorist Dave Barry once said, "To an adolescent, there is nothing more embarrassing in the world than a parent." And no, I'm not any cooler because I'm on "television." I'm still embarrassing to them, though thankfully not all the time.

But when my kids were four or five, they would always tug at me to play with them. If I kept begging them off, it would get worse. Until finally I said, okay, I will try to devote an hour every weeknight to just play only with them and shut everything else out. We're going to stick like glue and just play. After an hour, they would be satisfied that I had given them the attention they needed.

I realized that sometimes, all it takes is an hour or so of focus to really get what you need accomplished. So many of us are distracted by the day's tasks. I have the most annoying habit of talking and e-mailing at the same time, which drives people nuts because I'm not doing both well at all. But once in a while I remember I need to focus and when I do—say, spending an hour on tomorrow's show research—I always accomplish more than what I could in five hours' time. To be able to sequester yourself and focus is a powerful tool for productivity.

3. *Optimism.* Kids have a way of surprising us. I tend to think I'm a pretty optimistic person but sometimes even my kids trump me. When I worry about something, they're usually there with a few uplifting answers. The deer ate our vegetable patch? Don't worry, we'll just get a fence for next time. The power outage thanks to Hurricane Sandy means we have to spend four nights in the dark with no electricity or water? Well, at least we can tell ghost stories. The plane is delayed by two hours? Well now we can go get pizza. Sometimes I try to remember that whenever I find myself doing the thing that parents and lawyers tend to do, which is focus on the worst-case scenario. It usually takes a kid to lighten things up.

With the debate cleared in my head, I went on to think about what were the five most important things I learned from talking to the CEOs. If there were just five tips I could take away from this book and share with you, what would they be?

Below are the biggest:

1. Learn How to Make Fast Decisions . . . and Reverse Them if You Get New Information.

   Every single one of the CEOs is in that seat because he or she is a good decision maker. This is probably one of the most important skills any good leader possesses.

   Recall that Martin Sorrell, the advertising chief, had inscribed on his shield "Persistence and Speed." He said speed was related to how he views decision making.

   "I have a quote which was 'A bad decision on Monday is better than a good decision on Friday,' which was meant to say, 'Get on with it,'" Martin said. "I suppose that's my favorite phrase, 'Get on with it.' What bedevils big companies is a lack of response, failure to respond, bureaucracies that cogitate over things. The reason that people don't make decisions is because they're uncertain about that decision, or they don't know the answer. And my father used to say 'Delay is a negative,' and I think that's true. So when people don't make decisions, it's not because you have to take a long time to make the decision and there's a lot of information and data and analytics . . . [it's because] they're frightened of making decisions . . . if I don't make a decision, it's because I don't know what the answer is or I'm scared of the answer."

   Teresa Taylor put her interview subjects through lunch to see if they could make simple decisions about ordering. Fast decision making, she believes, is what got her into the senior ranks.

   "I didn't even know I was going to be in the telecom field so the whole thing was by circumstance," she said. "But I would say that I did have a drive and if I had to say what kept getting me the promotions, it was my decision-making capability. I think one of the areas that people falter on is they just can't make a decision. And especially as you're leading bigger groups, just make one, and then you can adjust as you go."

"Why do you think people have a hard time making decisions?" I asked.

"I think it's because people say . . . well, I just want to see a little bit more. It's the hesitation, the lack of confidence. And in fact, you never have all the pieces. When you're making decisions you work with what you have. You go through your instinct and your role. And I used to have a saying that, 'At least if we were in grenade range, it was good enough'. . . because no one is *that* perfect and things change and move and happen. So I think what contributed to my success was the ability to make a decision, be very clear and simple in my communication. So my teams knew what our goal was. It was clear. It was simple. And we charged forward and were successful."

Equally important is knowing when a decision you've made, based on new information, is bad and reversing it just as quickly. This is where people tend to get in trouble. Their egos get wrapped up in a decision and reversing it makes the person feel weak and vulnerable. It's tough to admit when you're wrong. Clearly you want to have more right than wrong decisions, but a hallmark of good leadership is knowing when something is not working and changing course.

One of the highlights in Warren Buffett's annual letters to his investors is when he admits he's made a bad investment decision. Rather than hang onto the stock to prove he's right, he explains why he has sold off the entire stake. Among the mistakes he's admitted to making in the last few years include paying too much for oil stocks and buying a shoe company that was later deemed worthless.

2. Have a Good Team Around You.

Every CEO has a close group of people around them, such as their senior management team, friends, or mentors. I noted before that it's a lonely job but it's not a job that's conducted in isolation.

Usually, the people around a CEO have been with him or her for decades. They're people they trust and grew up professionally with. Sometimes they may depend on certain people too much, such as when one CEO joked that he's met some fellow chief executives who "can't go to the bathroom without consulting their lawyer first."

It's important as you develop your career that you have a team of people you trust and are looking out for you. They don't necessarily have to be at your company and most times, they are not. They're not always senior to you and they may even be outside your own profession. They may not necessarily be more successful than you but they possess certain skills or knowledge you don't have. Elon Musk mentioned that he actively solicits negative feedback, which is the same thing as saying you want to have people around you who give honest feedback.

Tim Armstrong, the CEO of AOL, said National Basketball Association Commissioner David Stern—someone who many CEOs look up to for leadership—gives him "direct feedback."

"He called me up two Fridays ago and said, 'What are you doing, schmuck.' It was about some brand stuff. That's a sign of a great mentor—people who you trust will give you very direct feedback on things."

Having a good team also means having a good set of professionals around you—an accountant you can trust, a lawyer who advises well, a real estate broker who keeps you in the know on the market, and other people who keep you on track. You may not be able to assemble this right away but it's always a good idea to begin early and start getting recommendations from people. Who do they like to use? Who spends time without charging? Why do they like these people?

Who's Afraid of Sleep?

People often ask me what I notice when I interview high-powered people. What's a common trait?

When I really thought about it, one universal theme is: They all don't sleep that much.

The person who slept the most was Warren Buffett but even he, at the age of 82, was lacking. Buffett wrote in a note:

Probably average 6–7.
Sometimes 5.
Sometimes more than 10 on weekends.

According to the National Sleep Foundation, the average adult needs between seven to nine hours of sleep. But the foundation also recognizes that every individual is different. Some need just five hours to function well and others need closer to 10.

CEOs seem to sleep between five and six.

Sam Zell snoozes for six hours. Matin Sorrell said, "Five hours in the week. Catch up on weekends."

"I sleep around five to six hours a night . . . I'd love to sleep more but can't!" Tim Armstrong wrote.

Women do no better. Sallie Krawcheck wrote, "I sleep about six hours a night/seven on the weekends. On the weekends, I try for longer, but my body won't let me."

According to the Mayo Clinic, adults who consistently sleep less than seven hours a night have a higher mortality rate. Is it the lack of sleep that kills you or the stress that accompanies poor sleep?

Average Joes and Janes behave a little better. An article in the *New York Times* found that a third of adults slept about seven to eight hours, spot on with the recommendation by doctors and researchers.

But maybe we are stretching the truth. How many people really get a decent eight hours during the week? Even if you're in bed by 10 P.M., you might take an hour to fall asleep or wake up in the middle of the night. The reality is we're a nation of restless sleepers.

I used to sleep right at 8 P.M. for my 3:45 A.M. wake-up call. Nowadays, I'm lucky if I physically crawl into bed at 9. I kept a sleep diary one week and found that I usually get about five to five-and-a-half hours of sleep a weeknight, which I found very upsetting. I'm told trying to make up for sleep on the weekends is even worse.

My mission is to get more sleep. If there's one habit I *don't* want to pick up from the CEOs, it's that I need my beauty rest. And so should the rest of us.

Bad advice is free and everywhere. I'm always amazed at how people will make large, life-changing decisions based on advice from people they've barely vetted or from people who are not even qualified to give the advice. An accountant I know laments how many times clients ask for financial advice—getting financial planning advice from your accountant is like going to your mortgage broker to give you tips on investing in the housing market. But if you ask, you'll get the advice. Free.

3. Information Is Key.

This is not about hoarding information.

It's about being a voracious consumer of information.

This is easy for me to say because I'm in the business of information. We exchange and report on information all the time. Part of my job is to read everything and stay well informed.

Several CEOs I talked to recommended books to read. Jamie Dimon said he'd just finished Colin Powell's book *It Worked For Me.* Jim Reynolds was sitting on the beach reading *Good to Great* and *Built to Last* by Jim Collins for the "fourth or fifth time." Harry Wilson suggested *Halftime* by Bob Buford and *Enough.* by John Bogle. Sallie Krawcheck referred to *Women's Inhumanity to Women.* And so on.

Warren Buffett can sit in his office for hours reading annual reports and financial documents. Mario Gabelli walks around with a briefcase always brimming with research reports he wants to read. Every time he sits down in the studio chair with me he's got piles of papers around him, ready for referral. I start my day reading three to four newspapers.

The reason why this is important goes back to what Jim Reynolds called *bandwidth.* How much do you really know? How curious are you about the world around you? Can you sit in a room and relate to everyone—from the housewife from Texas to the mechanic in Detroit to the trader at the New York Stock Exchange. In other words, are you aware of the world around you?

The people who grow to be huge successes do not narrow the world around them but expand their field of vision. They can be great conversationalists because they know a little bit of everything that's going on. How many times have you been in a group and suddenly they are talking about a news event or subject matter that you know nothing about? You can't relate anymore. Having knowledge is so important—not only to be a well-rounded person but for relating to people.

One of the easiest ways to forge a connection with a person is to help inform them. E-mail your bosses news they may not know, and even if they know, they will appreciate getting the information. Don't pester but be helpful. I love it when our team constantly passes along news and tidbits to the group. I learn things I hadn't paid attention to before. When someone important sends you a link to a news article or a video, watch and read it and respond. People like to know you've paid attention. You don't have to do it to the degree I or others do, but if you just put a little effort into consuming information, making yourself well informed, being curious about the world around you, you'd be surprised at how the world opens up.

4. Have a Sense of Humor.

If I'm asked to give a talk or emcee an event, the first thing I think of is: Who is the audience and what jokes am I going to tell?

Humor is one of the most underrated skills in your career toolbox. One of the first things Sam Zell said made him a successful person is that he can laugh at himself. He doesn't take himself too seriously. All the CEOs I talked to possessed a great sense of humor, some funnier than others. They all understand an element in developing a relationship is laughing together. I have a very difficult time connecting myself to someone who can't get a joke. I try to relate to an audience by telling a few opening lines. If I can't come up with many on my own, I borrow from the Kings of Late Night Comedy.

Humor diffuses the serious tension in the air. When I saw General Colin Powell speak, his 45-minute speech was more than 80 percent filled with humorous stories. They were genuinely funny. At moments I found myself belly laughing. Nobody expected a serious four-star general to deliver punch lines almost as good as a stand-up comic. He had the room captivated for almost an hour.

Women can be just as funny as men, in different ways. The important thing is to see the lighter side of things when you can and know when to show it. Obviously in a serious meeting, it's inappropriate. But if you're in a one-on-one lunch with your boss, if a meeting is losing energy, if relations are strained between colleagues, humor can do wonders.

On our show, we try to find some lighter moments to laugh. A silly story may do the trick, or a joke between reporters and myself. We don't script them in but we can tell when we need to lighten up. Viewers want the serious news but they also need a break. The *Wall Street Journal* made famous its A-Hed column on the front page where the silliest story of the day is given the same reportage as all of its other news stories. That dose of humor in an otherwise pretty thick and straight newspaper adds wonders to its depth. In explaining this feature once, the *Journal* said, "That anyone serious enough about life to read the *Wall Street Journal* should also be wise enough to step back and consider life's absurdities."

A few years ago at Bloomberg TV, the newsroom was abuzz in excitement. We were getting ready to relaunch the channel and everybody had been rehearsing for weeks on end and on weekends. Each show was scrutinized carefully by producers, executive producers, and ultimately, by Andy Lack, the CEO of Bloomberg Multimedia (Andy is now Chairman of Bloomberg Multimedia). By the time it got to Andy's desk, the shows had to look ready for air.

As we were winding down rehearsals, one of the senior producers came up with a brilliant idea. He asked that Jon Erlichman, who's now our senior West Coast correspondent, Adam Johnson, our *Street Smart* anchor, and myself, make a spoof video for Andy. We rehearsed it as seriously as we rehearsed anything else, only this time we were rehearsing all the shots we knew Andy would not want.

In the scene, I would walk down the aisle talking into the camera while Jon popped out of nowhere to accompany me down the newsroom and then Adam joined in on my other side. We had to wait for the new glass studio sliding doors to open and the three of us squeezed through together. Then we all sat down at a preschool table and chairs to continue to discuss the day's stories.

When Andy first saw the opening scenes, he was a little agitated. These were all *exactly* what he had asked producers and directors not to do. But then as the scene unfolded, he squeezed out a smile and then his trademark huge, cracked laugh when he saw the end result. It was a genius way to break the tension the newsroom felt and, in many ways, helped cement the feeling that the relaunch was ready. If we could laugh at ourselves, then we really weren't that worried.

5. Always Be Moving.

I put this in again because I can't stress how important it is.

Perhaps the single biggest difference between those who make it to the very top and those who languish is that the former are always moving. They don't stop.

When I say moving, I don't necessarily mean physically, although you do have to actually be doing things.

I'll give an example but I won't use this person's name.

A senior executive I know left his job. The people he knew whispered about him, said he wasn't ready to leave yet, and that he hadn't prepared well. It was going to be difficult for him to start another business. I talked to him occasionally and every time I did, he mentioned this or that meeting he was attending, this or that discussion, this or that place he was flying off to. For obvious reasons, he couldn't disclose details. I got the sense he was spending his days talking to people, meeting, exchanging ideas, just moving around a lot to figure out the next step. It was hard to tell if he was making progress or running around in circles.

A few months later, he landed a big job and he sounded relieved on the phone. You could tell he felt he had something to prove and he proved it. Even at the stage when you're at the top, when you believe you've made it, you're still hustling. That never stops, so long as you want to stay in the game. As long as you're moving, you're going somewhere. Once you stop, you stay.

I'll give you another example.

Do you know the book *Who Moved My Cheese*?

The book is now 15 years old and has probably skipped the generation of Millennials today. But its lesson is still as relevant today as it was in the 1990s.

The story is about two groups—the littlepeople, Hem and Haw, and two mice, Sniff and Scurry, who are on the hunt for more cheese through a giant maze. The littlepeople are more talkers than doers—they reflect all that is neurotic about us, how we fear leaving the comforts of familiarity, how a setback will cause us to stop, how we talk ourselves out of what our gut is saying.

The mice are much simpler. They just keep moving and when they hit a wall, they turn around and move somewhere else. They keep moving, not overthinking why a certain path dead-ends or why a certain path leads to a room with no cheese. As you can imagine, by the time the fable is over, the two mice have found all the cheese in the world simply because they kept moving. One of the littlepeople has learned the same lesson, albeit at a slow pace, and it's left uncertain if the other littlepeople character has learned the path to greatness (and cheese).

I read and reread that book every once in a while to remind myself that one of the biggest ingredients for success is not to over-think and just keep moving.

Always

Be

Moving

. . . and you will get there.

Bibliography

Accenture, "The Path Forward," 2012, www.accenture.com/us-en/company/people/women/Pages/insight-womens-research-2012-path-forward.aspx.

Arango, Tim. "How the AOL-Time Warner Merger Went So Wrong." *New York Times*, January 10, 2010, www.nytimes.com/2010/01/11/business/media/11merger.html.

Barsh, Joanna and Lareine Yee. "Unlocking the Full Potential of Women in the US Economy." McKinsey Study on Women, April 2011, www.mckinsey.com/client_service/organization/latest_thinking/unlocking_the_full_potential.

Bass, Frank. "Mothers Turn Breadwinners for 40% of U.S. Households With Kids." Bloomberg, May 29, 2013, www.bloomberg.com/news/2013-05-29/mothers-turn-breadwinners-for-40-of-u-s-households-with-kids.html.

Boston College Center on Wealth and Philanthropy, "The Joys and Dilemmas of Wealth Study." *Wealth and the Commonwealth Newsletter*, February 2008, www.bc.edu/dam/files/research_sites/cwp/ssi/vol13.html#article1.bg1.

Branson, Richard. "Rules for Being a Good Negotiator." *Richard* (blog), September 20, 2012, www.virgin.com/richard-branson/rules-for-being-a-good-negotiator.

Brewer, Geoffrey. "Snakes Top List of Americans' Fears," Gallup News Service, March 19, 2001, www.gallup.com/poll/1891/snakes-top-list-americans-fears.aspx.

Carlson, Nicholas. "The VC Firm that Funded Facebook Explains How to Hire." *Business Insider*, February 9, 2013, www.businessinsider.com/the-vc-firm-that-funded-facebook-explains-how-to-hire-2013-2?op=1.

Carnevale, Anthony P., Stephen J. Rose, and Ban Cheah. "The College Payoff." The Georgetown University Center on Education and the Workforce, August 5, 2011, www9.georgetown.edu/grad/gppi/hpi/cew/pdfs/college-payoff-complete.pdf.

DeCurtis, Anthony. "Not a Businessman—a Business, Man." *Men's Health*, October 5, 2010, www.menshealth.com/best-life/not-businessman-business-man.

Edmondson Bell, Ella L.J. "Right Before Your Eyes." Harvard Symposium on Gender & Work, March 2013, www.hbs.edu/faculty/conferences/2013-w50-research-symposium/Documents/bell.pdf.

Edward Jones, "Supporting America's Entrepreneurs." 2012, https://www.edwardjones.com/en_US/index.html.

Geerdens, Inge. "I'm Not Balancing Work and Life and I Feel Great." LinkedIn, May 13, 2013, www.linkedin.com/today/post/article/20130513162515-44558-i-m-not-balancing-work-and-life-and-i-feel-great.

"Happy Planet Index." The New Economic Foundation, www.happyplanetindex.org

Harvard Medical School, National Comorbidity Survey, www.hcp.med.harvard.edu/ncs/index.php

Hewlett, Sylvia Ann. Center for Work-Life Policy, www.worklifepolicy.org/index.php/section/research_pubs

Hill, Graham. "Living With Less. A Lot Less." *New York Times*, March 9, 2013, www.nytimes.com/2013/03/10/opinion/sunday/living-with-less-a-lot-less.html.

Hymowitz, Carol and Cécile Daurat. "Best-Paid Women in S&P 500 Settle for Less Remuneration." Bloomberg, August 13, 2013, www.bloomberg.com/news/2013-08-13/best-paid-women-in-s-p-500-settle-for-less-with-18-gender-gap.html.

Ignatius, Adi. "From the Editor: The World's Top CEO." *Harvard Business Review*, January-February 2013, http://hbr.org/2013/01/the-worlds-top-ceo.

Liu, Betty. "America's Most Popular Chefs: Titans at the Table." *BloombergTV*, June 25, 2013, www.bloomberg.com/video/america-s-most-popular-chefs-titans-at-the-table-2WJoRWoGSoWlexMEfbDodQ.html.

National Sleep Foundation. "How Much Sleep Do We Really Need?" www.sleepfoundation.org/article/how-sleep-works/how-much-sleep-do-we-really-need.

OECD. "Life Satisfaction." OECD Better Life Index, www.oecdbetterlifeindex.org/topics/life-satisfaction.

Pradel, Dina W., Hannah Riley Bowles, and Kathleen L. McGinn. "When Gender Changes the Negotiation." *Harvard Business School Working Knowledge*, February 13, 2006, http://hbswk.hbs.edu/item/5207.html.

RHR International. "CEO Snapshot Survey." January 2012, www.rhrinternational.com/100127/pdf/rs/Snapshot-One-Pager-Statues-ONE.pdf.

Smith, Elliott Blair, and Phil Kuntz. "CEO Pay 1,795-to-1 Multiple of Wages Skirts U.S. Law." Bloomberg, April 30, 2013, www.bloomberg.com/news/2013-04-30/ceo-pay-1-795-to-1-multiple-of-workers-skirts-law-as-sec-delays.html.

Tilin, Andrew. "Where Are All the Men?" *Yoga Journal*, March 2007, www.yogajournal.com/lifestyle/2585.

UBS. "What Is 'Wealthy?'" *Investor Watch*, 3Q 2013, www.ubs.com/content/dam/WealthManagementAmericas/documents/investor-watch-3Q2013-report.pdf.

United States Department of Labor, "Mass Layoff Statistics," Bureau of Labor Statistics, www.bls.gov/mls.

United States Department of Labor. "Quits Levels and Rates by Industry and Region, Seasonally Adjusted." Bureau of Labor Statistics, www.bls.gov/news.release/jolts.t04.htm.

Wang, Wendy, Kim Parker, and Paul Taylor. "Breadwinner Moms." Pew Research Social & Demographic Trends, May 29, 2013, www.pewsocialtrends.org/2013/05/29/breadwinner-moms.

Welch, Liz. "How I Live With Myself After Firing a Third of My Employees." *Inc.*, July/August 2013, www.inc.com/magazine/201307/liz-welch/how-i-live-with-myself-after-firing.html.

Wood, Graeme. "Secret Fears of the Super-Rich." *The Atlantic*, April 2011, www.theatlantic.com/magazine/archive/2011/04/secret-fears-of-the-super-rich/308419.

About the Author

Betty Liu is an award-winning reporter and television anchor who has covered business for over 15 years. She is currently the host of the morning program *In the Loop*, on Bloomberg Television, *In the Loop at the Half* on Bloomberg Radio and an ABC News contributor. Betty has written for the *Wall Street Journal*, the *Financial Times*, the *Far Eastern Economic Review*, and several other publications. Her first book, *Age Smart*, was published in 2006. She's a member of the Council on Foreign Relations and the Economic Club of New York. Betty hails from Philadelphia, which means she will drive very far for a Wawa hoagie. She lives in New Jersey.

Index